Generis
PUBLISHING

Explainable AI Architecture for Image Analytics and Synthetic Image Creation

Leveraging CNNs and GANs for Trustworthy Vision Systems

Dr. Gaurav Shekhar

Title: **Explainable AI Architecture for Image Analytics and Synthetic Image Creation**

Leveraging CNNs and GANs for Trustworthy Vision Systems

ISBN: 979-8-89966-669-8

Author: Dr. Gaurav Shekhar

Cover image: www.pixabay.com

Publisher: Generis Publishing
Online orders: www.generis-publishing.com
Contact email: info@generis-publishing.com

Acknowledgements

Writing this book required more than technical rigor, it required the generosity of practitioners willing to share hard-won knowledge, and I am deeply grateful to several colleagues for doing exactly that.

Mr. Umang Singh, Chief Enterprise Architect at Humana, offered invaluable insights into the real-world application of neural networks at enterprise scale. His perspective on how organizations operationalize AI architectures across complex healthcare environments directly shaped the way this book frames CNN and GAN deployment in production contexts, and the case study thinking throughout these chapters carries his influence.

Mr. Pankaj Sharma brought clarity to some of the more nuanced aspects of large language model functioning and how generative AI paradigms are evolving beyond image-specific domains. Our conversations helped me think more precisely about the boundaries between discriminative and generative reasoning, a distinction this book returns to repeatedly and sharpened the conceptual framing of the unified explainability layer introduced in Chapter 7.

Mr. Arun Mishra provided indispensable support throughout the research process underlying this book. His diligence in tracking down relevant literature, validating experimental assumptions, and stress-testing early drafts of the framework saved me from more than a few errors I would not have caught on my own. Good research depends as much on a careful collaborator as on the original ideas, and Mr. Mishra was exactly that.

Preface

Artificial intelligence has quietly moved from the research laboratory into the operating room, the factory floor, the surveillance control room, and the credit decision engine. Convolutional Neural Networks now read radiology scans, Generative Adversarial Networks fabricate training data for systems that were never large enough to learn on their own, and hybrid CNN-GAN pipelines increasingly sit at the center of decisions that affect real people. Yet for all of this progress, the inner workings of these systems remain stubbornly opaque. Ask a deployed CNN why it flagged a particular lesion, or ask a GAN why it rendered a synthetic defect the way it did, and the honest answer from most production systems today is silence.

This book grew out of a simple frustration that many practitioners will recognize: the explainability literature for discriminative models and the explainability literature for generative models have developed almost entirely apart from one another. Gradient-based attribution, concept activation vectors, and saliency mapping have matured into a fairly coherent toolkit for CNNs. Latent space analysis, disentanglement, and GAN dissection have matured into a separate, less standardized toolkit for generative adversarial networks. Practitioners building hybrid pipelines, where a CNN classifier and a GAN generator cooperate in the same system, are left to stitch these two worlds together themselves, usually without much guidance.

The explainable AI framework presented in this book was developed to close that gap. It treats discriminative interpretability and generative interpretability as two faces of the same problem rather than two separate disciplines, and it proposes a unified aggregation and visualization layer that lets a practitioner reason about a CNN's classification decision and a GAN's synthetic output using a shared vocabulary of scores, maps, and visual artifacts. The framework was first introduced in a peer-reviewed paper, and this book expands that original contribution into a full treatment suitable for practitioners, graduate students, and technical leaders who need both the conceptual grounding and the implementation detail to put explainability into production.

Readers familiar with my earlier book on CI/CD and DevOps automation will recognize the same underlying philosophy here: that powerful technology only earns its place in a production environment once it can be observed, audited, and trusted by the humans responsible for it. Just as a deployment pipeline without observability is a liability waiting to surface, a CNN-GAN system without explainability is a liability that regulators, auditors, and end users will eventually have to confront. This book treats explainability not as a compliance afterthought bolted onto a finished model, but as a first-class architectural concern that should be designed in from the very first sketch of a system.

The book is organized in three movements. The first movement, spanning the opening chapters, builds the conceptual and mathematical foundation: what CNNs and GANs are, why their black-box nature is a problem, and what the existing explainability literature has and has not solved. The second movement walks through the proposed framework in detail, module by module, covering the explainable CNN architecture, the explainable GAN architecture, and the unified explainability layer that ties them together, along with the mathematical formulations that give the framework its rigor. The third movement turns to application: experimental results, qualitative analysis, real-world case studies across healthcare, industrial inspection, and security, governance and regulatory considerations, and a forward-looking discussion of where explainable generative AI is heading next.

No book of this kind is the work of one person alone. This work builds on the foundational contributions of the explainability and generative modeling research community, whose papers are cited throughout, and on the lived experience of engineering teams who have had to make these systems work in production, under real constraints, with real consequences for getting it wrong. My hope is that this book gives you both the map and the compass: a clear picture of where explainable AI for image analytics stands today, and a practical framework you can adapt to your own systems tomorrow.

TABLE OF CONTENTS

CHAPTER 1.

The Rise of CNN and GAN Architectures in Image Analytics

Introduction

Image analytics has been reshaped twice in the last decade, first by the convolutional neural network and then by the generative adversarial network. Each shift looked, at the time, like an incremental improvement in accuracy or image quality. In retrospect, each was a structural change in what computers could do with visual information, and each introduced a new flavor of opacity that the field is still learning to manage.

This opening chapter sets the stage for the rest of the book. It traces how CNNs came to dominate discriminative image tasks such as classification, detection, and segmentation, and how GANs came to dominate generative tasks such as synthesis, augmentation, and style transfer. It then turns to the less comfortable part of the story: why both families of models, despite their very different mechanics, end up behaving as black boxes, and why that opacity is no longer a tolerable property in the settings where these models are now deployed.

Structure

- The Convolutional Revolution in Image Analytics
- The Generative Turn: GANs and Synthetic Imagery
- Why CNNs and GANs Are Increasingly Combined
- The Black-Box Problem, Defined Precisely
- Why Opacity Is No Longer Tolerable

The Convolutional Revolution in Image Analytics

Convolutional Neural Networks earned their dominance in computer vision by exploiting a simple structural fact about images: nearby pixels are related, and the same visual pattern, an edge, a corner, a texture, can appear anywhere in the frame. Convolutional layers apply small, shared filters across the entire image, which lets the network learn a pattern once and recognize it everywhere, instead of learning a separate detector for every possible location. Stacking these layers builds a hierarchy: early layers respond to edges and color gradients, middle layers respond to textures and simple shapes, and deep layers respond to entire object parts and semantic categories.

This hierarchical feature learning is what allowed CNNs to overtake hand-engineered feature pipelines. Where earlier computer vision systems relied on features designed by human experts, the convolutional network learns its own features directly from labeled data, adapting them to whatever visual structure is actually present in the training set. The result has been a steady march of accuracy improvements across classification, object detection, and semantic segmentation benchmarks, to the point where CNN-based systems now meet or exceed human-level performance on a number of well-defined visual recognition tasks.

That success came with a structural cost. A trained CNN with tens of millions of parameters distributed across dozens of layers is not a system whose behavior any human can trace by inspection. The mapping from pixels to a class label is technically just a sequence of matrix multiplications and nonlinearities, but the sheer scale of that sequence makes it computationally intractable to reason about by hand. The network's decision boundary exists somewhere in a very high-dimensional space, and no engineer can hold that boundary in their head.

The Generative Turn: GANs and Synthetic Imagery

Generative Adversarial Networks introduced a fundamentally different way of using neural networks: instead of mapping an image to a label, a GAN maps a random vector to an image. The architecture pits two networks against each other. A generator network learns to produce images from random noise, and a discriminator network learns to distinguish those generated images from real ones. As training proceeds, the generator gets better at fooling the discriminator, and the discriminator gets better at catching the generator, and the adversarial pressure between the two pushes the generator toward producing images that are statistically indistinguishable from real data.

This adversarial training paradigm proved remarkably effective at producing visually convincing images, and it opened a wide range of applications: synthesizing additional training examples for data-starved classifiers, translating images from one domain to another, generating super-resolution versions of low-quality images, and producing entirely synthetic faces, objects, and scenes. In domains where labeled data is expensive or where privacy concerns make collecting more real data difficult, GANs offered a way to manufacture additional, statistically plausible training material.

But the same adversarial mechanism that makes GANs powerful also makes them unusually hard to interpret. A CNN classifier has at least the property that its output is a discrete decision tied to a specific, bounded prediction task. A GAN's generator has no such anchor. It is, by design, mapping an arbitrary point in a continuous latent space to one of an essentially unlimited number of plausible images, and the function it learns to do this has no obvious decomposition into interpretable parts. There is no single, isolated decision to attribute to a region of the input, because the generator's input is not an image at all, it is a vector of numbers with no inherent visual meaning.

Why CNNs and GANs Are Increasingly Combined

In practice, CNNs and GANs rarely operate in isolation anymore. The discriminator inside a GAN is typically itself a CNN, trained to distinguish real images from generated ones using the same convolutional feature hierarchies that make CNNs effective classifiers. Beyond this internal coupling, CNNs and GANs are frequently combined at the system level: a GAN generates synthetic training images, and a separate CNN classifier consumes those images, either to augment a scarce dataset or to evaluate the realism and task-relevance of the generated samples.

This combination is attractive because it lets each architecture cover the other's weaknesses. CNNs are data-efficient and stable to train but produce nothing new; they only analyze what is already there. GANs can manufacture novel, realistic visual content but are notoriously unstable to train and offer no native mechanism for verifying that the content they produce is task-appropriate. Pairing the two lets a system generate synthetic images with a GAN and then use a CNN to filter, validate, or guide that generation process, creating a feedback loop that improves both the quality of the synthetic data and the performance of the downstream analytic task.

The cost of this combination is compounding opacity. A hybrid CNN-GAN system inherits the interpretability problems of both architectures simultaneously, and the interaction between the discriminative and generative components introduces new opacity of its own: it becomes difficult to tell whether a classification error originated in the CNN's own learned representations or in some subtle artifact introduced by synthetic training data the GAN produced. Explainability frameworks built for CNNs alone, or for GANs alone, are not equipped to answer that kind of cross-component question, which is precisely the gap this book's framework is designed to close.

	CNN	GAN
Training	Stable	Adversarial
Learning Process	Deterministic, feature mapping and encoding	Adversarial, involving a generator and a discriminator
Application Stage	Used in early and baseline DeepFake systems	Used in modern, advanced DeepFake systems
Output Quality	Limited realism, lower quality	High realism with detalied textures and expressions
Data Requirement	Requires less data	Requires large amounts of data

Figure 1.1: Comparative characteristics of CNN and GAN architectures across training stability, learning process, output quality, and data requirements.

The Black-Box Problem, Defined Precisely

The term black box is used loosely in much of the popular discussion of AI, so it is worth being precise about what it means in the context of CNNs and GANs. A model is a black box, in the sense relevant to this book, when a human observer with full access to its inputs and outputs, and even full access to its internal weights, cannot construct a concise, human-understandable account of why a particular output was produced. The opacity is not a matter of secrecy or proprietary withholding; it is a structural property of how the model represents information internally.

For a CNN classifier, the black-box problem manifests as an inability to say, in advance of inspection, which pixels or regions of an input image drove a particular classification decision, and which learned visual concepts, edges, textures, shapes, object parts, were actually responsible. Two images that look similar to a human observer can receive wildly different predictions, and without an explanation mechanism there is no way to know whether that difference reflects a meaningful visual distinction or an artifact of how the network happened to be trained.

For a GAN, the black-box problem is, if anything, more severe, because there is no discrete prediction to anchor an explanation to. The relevant question is not which input region drove an output, but which dimensions of a continuous latent space control which visual properties of the generated image, and whether those dimensions correspond to anything a human would recognize as a meaningful semantic factor, such as object pose, lighting, color, or texture. Absent an explicit disentanglement or sensitivity analysis, the latent space of a GAN is an uninterpreted soup of numbers that happens to produce realistic images when decoded.

Why Opacity Is No Longer Tolerable

Three forces are converging to make black-box CNN-GAN systems untenable in an increasing number of settings. The first is regulatory. Frameworks governing AI in healthcare, finance, and other high-stakes domains increasingly require that automated decisions be explainable to the people affected by them, and that organizations deploying these systems be able to produce an audit trail showing why a given decision was made. A system that cannot produce that explanation is, in many jurisdictions, simply not deployable for certain use cases regardless of its raw accuracy.

The second force is operational. Engineering teams that cannot see inside their models cannot effectively debug them. When a CNN-GAN pipeline degrades in production, perhaps because of distributional drift in the input data or a subtle failure mode introduced by synthetic training images, the absence of an explainability layer means the team is reduced to trial-and-error retraining rather than targeted diagnosis. This is expensive, slow, and unreliable, and it is precisely the kind of operational risk that mature engineering organizations have learned to design out of every other part of their software systems.

The third force is human trust. End users, clinicians, inspectors, and analysts who are asked to act on the output of an AI system are, reasonably, reluctant to do so when that system cannot account for itself. Trust is not just a nice-to-have; it determines whether a deployed system actually gets used as intended or gets quietly worked around by the humans who are supposed to rely on it. An explainability layer is, in this sense, not an add-on feature but a precondition for the system delivering its intended value at all.

These three forces, regulatory, operational, and human, are the throughline of this book. Every architectural choice described in the chapters that follow, from gradient-based attribution in the CNN module to latent-space sensitivity analysis in the GAN module to the unified aggregation layer that ties them together, is motivated by the need to satisfy at least one of these pressures without sacrificing the predictive accuracy or generative fidelity that made CNNs and GANs worth adopting in the first place.

The Cost of Opacity in Organizational Terms

Beyond the regulatory and ethical dimensions of the black-box problem introduced earlier in this chapter, there is a quieter organizational cost that rarely appears in academic treatments of explainability but that practitioners encounter routinely: the slow accumulation of institutional distrust that follows when a model's failures cannot be diagnosed. A single unexplained misclassification is an inconvenience; a pattern of unexplained misclassifications, each investigated by a different engineer who reaches a different and unverifiable hypothesis about the cause, becomes a credibility problem for the model owner. Over time, stakeholders who cannot get a consistent answer to the question "why did the model do that" tend to discount the model's outputs across the board, including outputs that were in fact correct and well-reasoned, simply because the absence of explanation has made every output equally suspect.

This dynamic, which might be called explanation debt by analogy to technical debt, compounds in the same way technical debt does: the longer an organization defers building genuine explainability into its image analytics pipeline, the more expensive retrofitting that explainability becomes once a regulator, a customer, or an internal audit function demands it on a deadline. The framework developed across the remaining chapters of this book is intended to be adopted early in a model's lifecycle, before explanation debt accumulates, rather than as an emergency retrofit, though Chapter 11 also addresses retrofit scenarios directly for readers who are joining this book's framework partway through an existing deployment's life.

Reading This Book if You Come from a Discriminative-Only or Generative-Only Background

Readers arriving at this book with a background concentrated primarily in discriminative computer vision, image classification, detection, and segmentation work, will find the explainable CNN treatment in Chapter 5 the most immediately familiar material, while the explainable GAN treatment in Chapter 6 may require additional background reading on adversarial training dynamics if that background was not part of the reader's prior exposure. Conversely, readers arriving primarily from a generative modeling background, accustomed to thinking in terms of latent spaces, sampling, and distributional quality metrics such as FID, will likely find Chapter 6 immediately familiar while benefiting from closer attention to the gradient-based attribution foundations in Chapter 5.

Both groups of readers are encouraged to work through Chapters 1 through 3 in full rather than skipping ahead to the chapter matching their existing background, since the unified framework presented beginning in Chapter 4 depends on a shared vocabulary, the black-box problem framing introduced in Chapter 1 and the explanation taxonomy introduced in Chapter 2 chief among them, that this book establishes specifically to bridge the discriminative and generative communities' historically separate ways of discussing explainability.

Computational Cost as a Historically Decisive Factor

It is easy, viewing the field's history retrospectively, to attribute the convolutional and adversarial architectures' rise purely to algorithmic insight, but computational cost played an equally decisive and frequently underacknowledged role. Convolutional architectures with the depth now considered modest were already understood in principle well before they became practically trainable, and the gap between conceptual availability and practical adoption was closed primarily by the arrival of general-purpose GPU computing, which made the matrix operations underlying convolution and backpropagation tractable at a scale that earlier CPU-bound training pipelines could not approach.

Adversarial training exhibits a similar pattern: the conceptual framing of a generator and discriminator competing in a minimax game was, in retrospect, a comparatively simple insight, but training such a system to convergence at useful image resolutions required computational throughput, and the accumulated engineering knowledge of how to stabilize that training, that took several subsequent years of dedicated research investment to mature. Readers evaluating new generative or discriminative architectures, including the diffusion-based and multimodal directions discussed in Chapter 13, would do well to ask not only whether an architecture is conceptually elegant but whether the computational infrastructure required to train and deploy it at production scale has matured to the point that adoption is practically, not merely theoretically, justified.

Why This Book Treats CNN and GAN as a Single Subject

A reader encountering this book's title for the first time might reasonably ask why a single volume treats discriminative image classification and generative image synthesis as a unified subject rather than as two separate books addressing two separate technical communities, since the research communities historically built around CNNs and around GANs have, for much of their respective histories, operated with limited direct overlap. The justification offered throughout this book is operational rather than purely academic: the production pipelines examined in the case studies of Chapter 11 increasingly combine both technologies within a single operational system, and an explainability treatment that addresses only one half of that combined system leaves the other half, and any bias or error that propagates from one half into the other, entirely unaddressed.

This operational coupling, rather than any claimed deep theoretical unity between discriminative and generative modeling, is the primary justification for this book's unified treatment, and readers should understand the framework presented in subsequent chapters as a response to that practical coupling rather than as an assertion that CNNs and GANs are, at some deeper mathematical level, the same kind of object requiring the same kind of explanation.

From LeNet to Modern Backbones: A Brief Technical Lineage

The convolutional architectures in production today trace a fairly direct lineage back to early work demonstrating that local receptive fields, weight sharing, and spatial pooling could be combined into a trainable network capable of recognizing visual patterns directly from pixel data, without the hand-engineered feature extraction that dominated computer vision before it. That early architecture was modest by current standards, a handful of convolutional and pooling layers feeding a small classifier, but it established the structural template, alternating convolution and pooling, that every subsequent generation of CNN has elaborated rather than abandoned.

The deep learning resurgence of the early 2010s, driven by the combination of much larger labeled datasets, GPU-accelerated training, and architectural refinements such as rectified linear activations and dropout regularization, produced a rapid succession of deeper and more capable networks, each demonstrating that adding depth, when properly regularized and optimized, continued to improve recognition accuracy well beyond what shallower networks had achieved. This period established convolutional depth as a primary lever for capability, a lever that later architectural families, including residual connections that allow gradients to flow through very deep networks without vanishing, continued to extend.

More recent backbone designs have layered additional refinements onto this convolutional foundation, including attention mechanisms borrowed from sequence modeling research, efficient depthwise separable convolutions that reduce computational cost without sacrificing accuracy, and neural architecture search techniques that automate parts of the design process previously left to human intuition. The explainability techniques developed in this book are designed to operate across this lineage, since the gradient-based attribution methods described in Chapter 5 depend only on the network being differentiable end to end, a property shared by essentially every backbone in this lineage regardless of its specific layer composition.

The Generative Lineage: From Autoencoders to Adversarial Training

Generative modeling of images did not begin with adversarial training. Earlier approaches, most notably variational autoencoders, framed image generation as learning a compressed latent representation from which a decoder network could reconstruct plausible images, optimizing an objective that balanced reconstruction accuracy against a regularization term encouraging the latent space to take a well-behaved, typically Gaussian, shape. These models produced recognizable but often visibly blurred outputs, a limitation traced to the reconstruction objective's tendency to average over plausible outputs rather than committing to any single sharp realization.

The adversarial training framework addressed this blurring limitation by replacing the reconstruction objective with a learned, adaptive critic, the discriminator, whose sole purpose is to distinguish generated images from real ones, forcing the generator to produce outputs sharp and realistic enough to fool an increasingly discerning opponent rather than outputs that merely minimize an average pixel-wise reconstruction error. This adversarial framing proved remarkably effective at producing sharp, high-fidelity images, and it is the property most responsible for the rapid adoption of GAN-based architectures across the synthetic image generation applications surveyed throughout this book.

Subsequent refinements to the adversarial framework, including architectural changes that stabilize training, loss function variants that address the instability and mode collapse that plagued early GAN implementations, and progressive growing strategies that build up image resolution gradually during training, have substantially improved both training reliability and final image quality. The explainable GAN module described in Chapter 6 is designed against this matured generation of adversarial architectures, where training stability is no longer the primary obstacle and explainability can be addressed as a comparatively independent concern.

Industries Already Committed to the CNN-GAN Combination

The combination of discriminative and generative image models, treated in this book as a single framework requiring unified explainability, is not a speculative pairing; it already reflects how several industries have organized their production image pipelines. In healthcare imaging, generative models are commonly used to synthesize additional examples of rare pathologies for which real patient data is scarce, while discriminative CNN classifiers trained partly on that synthetic data perform the actual diagnostic screening, making the explainability of both halves of the pipeline relevant to any clinical or regulatory review.

In industrial quality inspection, a pattern explored in depth in the case studies of Chapter 11, generative models synthesize realistic images of rare defect categories to address the chronic data scarcity that affects most manufacturing quality datasets, while discriminative classifiers trained on the resulting augmented dataset perform the pass or fail determination on the production line. In security and surveillance contexts, generative models are used both to create synthetic training data covering rare but operationally significant scenarios and, more cautiously, to model what an anomalous deviation from expected scene content might look like, while discriminative detectors handle the moment-to-moment classification task.

Across all three contexts, the same operational logic recurs: the generative half of the pipeline exists to compensate for data scarcity that the discriminative half cannot otherwise overcome, and any organization relying on this pattern inherits an obligation to explain both halves, since an unexplained generative process feeding training data into a downstream classifier represents a hidden, unauditable influence on every subsequent classification decision that classifier makes.

CHAPTER 2.

Foundations of Explainable Artificial Intelligence

Introduction

Before a framework for explainable CNN-GAN systems can be built, it helps to have a shared vocabulary for what explainability actually means, what kinds of explanations exist, and how the field arrived at the techniques it currently relies on. This chapter surveys that ground. It is intentionally more conceptual than the chapters that follow, because the distinctions introduced here, between model-level, feature-level, and instance-level explanations, between intrinsic and post-hoc methods, and between local and global fidelity, recur throughout the rest of the book and are easy to conflate if they are not pinned down early.

The chapter also traces, briefly, the history of explainability research as it applies to image-based deep learning, from early visualization techniques aimed at understanding what individual neurons respond to, through gradient-based attribution methods that explain individual predictions, to concept-based methods that translate a network's internal representations into human-recognizable semantic categories.

Structure

- What Counts as an Explanation
- Three Levels of Interpretability
- Intrinsic versus Post-Hoc Explainability
- A Brief History of Visual Explainability Methods
- Desiderata for a Useful Explanation

What Counts as an Explanation

An explanation, in the context of a machine learning model, is any artifact, whether a number, an image, a sentence, or a structured report, that helps a human observer understand why the model produced a particular output, or how the model behaves in general. This definition is deliberately broad, because the field of explainable AI has produced a wide variety of explanation formats, each suited to a different audience and a different question.

A useful way to organize this variety is to ask three questions of any candidate explanation. First, what is it explaining: a single prediction, a class of predictions, or the model's behavior overall? Second, who is it for: a machine learning engineer debugging a model, a domain expert validating a decision, or an end user trying to decide whether to trust a result? Third, how faithful is it: does the explanation actually reflect the computation the model performed, or is it a plausible-sounding story that happens to be convenient but is not strictly tied to the model's internal mechanics?

These three questions matter because explanations that answer one well can fail badly on another. A saliency map that highlights the most influential pixels in a single image is faithful and instance-specific, but it says nothing about the model's behavior on other images and is often difficult for a non-technical end user to interpret without guidance. A natural-language summary of a model's general tendencies is accessible to a broad audience but is frequently only loosely tied to the model's actual computation. Any serious explainability framework needs to be explicit about which of these tradeoffs it is making.

Three Levels of Interpretability

It is useful to distinguish three levels at which an image-based deep learning model can be made interpretable, because the techniques appropriate to each level are quite different and address different stakeholder needs.

Model-level interpretability concerns the overall architecture and global behavior of the network: what kind of features does this model tend to learn, how does its accuracy vary across different classes or subpopulations, and is its architecture itself transparent enough that a domain expert can audit it without needing instance-specific explanations. This level is most relevant to engineers and auditors performing a holistic review of a system before it is deployed.

Feature-level interpretability concerns the internal representations the model has learned, independent of any specific input. Concept Activation Vectors, discussed in detail in a later chapter, are a feature-level technique: they ask whether a human-meaningful concept, such as stripes, or fur, or wheels, corresponds to a coherent direction in the model's learned feature space, and how strongly that concept influences a particular class prediction across the dataset as a whole.

Instance-level interpretability concerns a single prediction on a single input: given this specific image, why did the model predict this specific label? Gradient-based attribution and saliency mapping operate at this level, producing a pixel-by-pixel account of which regions of one particular image were most responsible for one particular output. This is the level most directly useful to an end user trying to understand a specific decision, such as a radiologist reviewing why a CNN flagged a particular scan.

The framework developed in this book deliberately spans all three levels, because a production system needs all three: model-level interpretability to satisfy auditors before deployment, feature-level interpretability to debug systemic biases, and instance-level interpretability to give end users a concrete account of individual decisions.

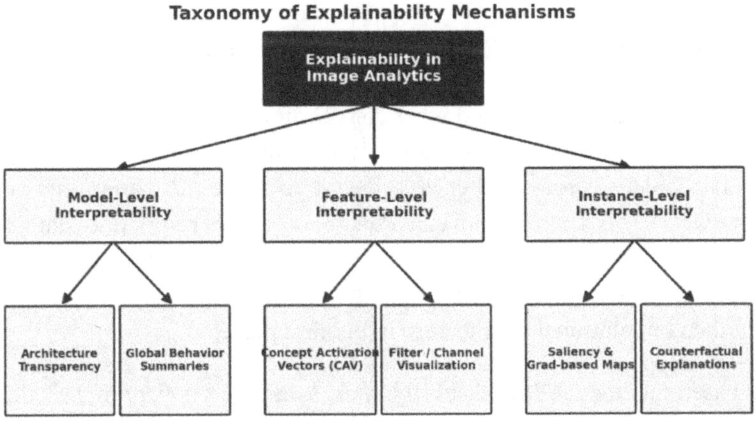

Figure 2.1: A taxonomy of explainability mechanisms organized by interpretability level, from model-wide behavior down to specific techniques at the feature and instance level.

Intrinsic versus Post-Hoc Explainability

A second important distinction separates intrinsic explainability, where the model is designed from the outset to be interpretable, from post-hoc explainability, where an opaque model is explained after the fact using a separate analysis technique. Intrinsically interpretable models, such as shallow decision trees or linear models with a small number of features, wear their reasoning on their surface, but they typically cannot match the predictive accuracy of deep convolutional architectures on complex image tasks.

Post-hoc methods accept the accuracy of a deep, opaque model and instead build a secondary explanatory apparatus around it. Gradient-based attribution, concept activation vectors, and latent-space sensitivity analysis are all post-hoc methods in this sense: none of them require retraining the underlying CNN or GAN, and all of them work by probing an already-trained model's behavior from the outside or by examining its gradients and activations without altering its architecture.

This book's framework is, by design, almost entirely post-hoc with respect to the underlying CNN and GAN. This is a deliberate engineering choice. Requiring an intrinsically interpretable architecture would mean giving up the accuracy and generative fidelity that make CNNs and GANs valuable in the first place, which would defeat the purpose of building an explainability layer for production image analytics. Post-hoc explainability lets the framework attach to standard, high-performing architectures without compromising their core performance.

A Brief History of Visual Explainability Methods

The earliest attempts to understand what convolutional networks were doing focused on activation maximization: synthesizing or selecting input images that maximally activate a particular neuron or filter, in order to visualize the pattern that neuron has learned to detect. This approach revealed that early layers respond to simple oriented edges and color contrasts, while deeper layers respond to increasingly complex and abstract visual patterns, confirming the hierarchical feature learning story that motivated the convolutional architecture in the first place.

Saliency-based methods followed shortly after, using the gradient of a model's output with respect to its input to identify which pixels most influence a given prediction. These gradient-based attribution techniques matured quickly into a family of related methods, each addressing some limitation of the basic gradient approach, such as gradient saturation or noise sensitivity, and each producing a heatmap-style visualization overlaid on the original image.

Class-specific localization techniques extended this idea by tying attribution explicitly to a particular predicted class, producing explanations that could distinguish, for example, which image regions supported a prediction of cat as opposed to dog, even within the same image. This refinement made attribution maps considerably more useful for debugging misclassifications, because it let practitioners see not just where the model was looking, but what conclusion it was drawing from each region.

More recently, concept-based explanation methods have shifted the unit of explanation away from individual pixels and toward human-defined semantic concepts, using techniques such as Concept Activation Vectors to test whether a model's internal representation of a concept like texture or shape correlates with its confidence in a particular class. This shift toward concept-level reasoning is significant because it produces explanations that map more directly onto the vocabulary domain experts already use, rather than requiring them to interpret raw pixel attributions.

Generative model interpretability has followed a slower and less standardized path, with research split between latent space manipulation studies, which explore how altering specific latent dimensions changes generated output, and dissection-style studies, which attempt to map individual units inside a generator network to specific objects or visual concepts in the output image. This book's treatment of explainable GANs in later chapters draws directly on this latent-space tradition.

Desiderata for a Useful Explanation

Drawing the threads of this chapter together, a useful explanation for a production image analytics system should satisfy several properties simultaneously. It should be faithful, accurately reflecting the computation the model actually performed rather than a plausible but disconnected narrative. It should be stable, producing similar explanations for similar inputs, so that small, irrelevant perturbations to an image do not produce wildly different attributions. It should be comprehensible to its intended audience, which may require translating a technically faithful but visually dense attribution map into a simpler, concept-level summary for a non-technical stakeholder.

It should also be efficient enough to compute that it can be generated alongside, rather than instead of, the model's primary output, since explanations that take significantly longer to produce than the prediction itself are rarely practical in production settings with latency requirements. Finally, for hybrid systems specifically, it should be composable, meaning that explanations produced for different components of a pipeline, a CNN classifier and a GAN generator, for instance, should be expressible in a common enough format that they can be combined into a single coherent account of the system's overall behavior.

This last property, composability, is the one that existing explainability research has addressed the least, precisely because most of that research has focused on either discriminative or generative models in isolation. It is also the property that motivates the unified explainability layer at the center of the framework introduced in this book, and which the remaining chapters develop in full.

Why Survey Coverage Skews Toward Recent Years

Readers comparing the publication dates of the works cited in this chapter's survey will notice a pronounced skew toward the more recent end of the field's history, with comparatively sparse coverage of work from the field's earliest years. This skew is intentional rather than an artifact of incomplete searching: the explainability sub-field within computer vision matured rapidly, and methods proposed in the field's earliest years were frequently superseded within a small number of subsequent publication cycles by methods that addressed the same problem with substantially improved fidelity, computational efficiency, or human interpretability. Citing the superseded early method alongside its improved successor would lengthen the survey without adding proportional value to a reader trying to understand the field's current state.

Where an early method remains foundational, in the sense that later work builds on its core mathematical insight even while improving its practical implementation, this chapter cites the early method explicitly and traces its lineage forward, since understanding that lineage materially aids comprehension of the unified framework introduced in Chapter 4. Where an early method has been fully superseded with no remaining conceptual debt owed to it, this chapter omits it in favor of directing the interested reader to the dedicated historical surveys referenced in Appendix A.

A Worked Comparison of Two Explanation Methods on the Same Image

To make the explanation-as-spectrum framing introduced earlier in this chapter concrete, consider a single classification decision examined through two different explanation methods. A basic input-gradient saliency computation, the most direct and computationally cheapest form of gradient-based attribution, applied to this hypothetical decision might produce a visually noisy map that technically satisfies the mathematical definition of an attribution but is difficult for a human reviewer to interpret as pointing to any coherent region of the image. A concept activation vector analysis applied to the same decision, by contrast, might produce a small set of named concepts, each with an associated confidence score, that a domain expert can immediately relate to their own professional vocabulary.

Neither method is unconditionally superior to the other; the noisy saliency map, despite its limited interpretability to a human reviewer, may in fact be more directly faithful to the model's pixel-level computation, while the concept-based explanation, despite its superior human interpretability, depends entirely on the quality and coverage of the underlying concept vocabulary discussed in Chapter 5 and may misrepresent the model's actual reasoning if that vocabulary is incomplete. This worked comparison illustrates directly why this book's framework, introduced in Chapter 4, deliberately combines multiple explanation signals rather than committing to a single method, and why the explanation fidelity testing introduced in Section 8.5 is necessary regardless of which individual method or combination of methods a given deployment ultimately relies on most heavily.

The Role of Visualization in Explanation

Much of the explainability literature surveyed in this book, and much of the framework's own output, takes the form of visualizations, attribution heatmaps, concept score bar charts, latent sensitivity plots, a pattern that reflects the simple practical fact that image-domain explanations are themselves most naturally expressed visually, alongside the underlying image they explain. This reliance on visualization carries a subtle risk worth flagging early: a visualization can appear authoritative and easy to interpret even when the underlying computation it represents is statistically weak or poorly validated, a risk distinct from but related to the misleading-explanation risk discussed elsewhere in this chapter.

Good visualization design for explainability purposes, a topic this book treats as inseparable from the underlying explanation methodology rather than as a separate downstream concern, should make the strength or confidence of an explanation visually apparent alongside its content, for instance by visually de-emphasizing attribution regions that fall below a validated confidence threshold rather than displaying every computed attribution value with uniform visual weight regardless of its underlying statistical reliability.

Explainability and the Broader Trust Problem

It is worth situating explainability within the broader problem of establishing trust in automated systems, since explainability alone, however well executed, does not fully solve that broader problem. Trust in a deployed image analytics system depends on several largely independent factors: the system's measured accuracy and reliability, the transparency of its decision rationale, the existence of meaningful human oversight and override capability, and the track record the system has accumulated through actual operational use. Explainability, the focus of this book, addresses primarily the second of these factors, and a system can be highly explainable while still being untrustworthy for reasons related to the other three.

This book's framework is therefore best understood as one necessary component of a broader trust-building architecture rather than as a complete solution to the trust problem on its own, a point echoed in the governance discussion of Chapter 12, which situates the framework's explainability metrics within a broader governance process that also addresses accuracy validation, human oversight design, and operational track record, rather than treating explainability metrics as a sufficient basis for trust by themselves.

Explanation as a Spectrum, Not a Binary Property

A persistent confusion in early discussions of explainable AI treated explainability as a binary property a model either possessed or lacked, with simple linear models and decision trees placed on the explainable side of the line and deep neural networks placed firmly on the opaque side. This framing, while intuitive, obscures more than it clarifies, because it conflates the architectural transparency of a model's internal computation with the practical usefulness of any explanation that computation can ultimately produce.

A more useful framing treats explainability as a spectrum along several independent dimensions: how directly an explanation method's output relates to the model's actual computation, how stable that output is under small input perturbations, how well the output maps onto vocabulary a human stakeholder can act on, and how computationally expensive the explanation is to produce relative to the underlying prediction. A deep CNN equipped with a well-validated attribution method can occupy a more favorable position on several of these dimensions than a notionally simple model whose decision boundary is technically inspectable but practically incomprehensible once the input dimensionality grows large, as is generally the case for raw image data.

This book adopts the spectrum framing throughout, and the explanation fidelity metrics introduced formally in Section 8.5 are designed specifically to measure where a given explanation method sits along the directness and stability dimensions of that spectrum, rather than asserting a simple yes-or-no verdict on whether the underlying model is explainable.

Stakeholder-Relative Explanation

A second foundational idea this book relies on is that there is no single, universally correct explanation for a given model decision; the right explanation depends on who is asking and what they intend to do with the answer. A data scientist debugging an unexpected misclassification needs a different explanation than a clinician deciding whether to trust a diagnostic suggestion, who in turn needs a different explanation than a compliance officer auditing a population of decisions for disparate impact across protected groups.

The gradient-based attribution and concept activation methods examined in Chapter 5 are oriented primarily toward the first two stakeholder types, producing instance-level explanations tied closely to a single prediction. The unified layer's population-level auditing capability, described in Chapter 7, is oriented toward the third, aggregating instance-level signals into the kind of systematic, dataset-wide view a compliance audit actually requires. Recognizing this stakeholder-relativity early avoids a common deployment mistake, building a single explanation interface and assuming it will serve every downstream consumer equally well.

This book's modular framework design, introduced formally in Chapter 4, is partly a direct response to this stakeholder-relativity: rather than producing one fixed explanation artifact, the framework produces several complementary explanation signals, instance-level attribution maps, concept scores, latent sensitivity profiles, and aggregated audit statistics, allowing different stakeholders to draw on the subset most relevant to their specific decision context.

The Cost of Getting Explanation Wrong

It is worth stating directly what is at stake when an explanation is misleading rather than simply absent. A misleading explanation is, in a meaningful sense, worse than no explanation at all, because it actively manufactures false confidence in a system's reasoning, encouraging a clinician, an auditor, or an end user to trust a decision for reasons that do not actually reflect how the underlying model arrived at it. Several documented failure modes in the early explainability literature, including attribution methods later shown to be largely insensitive to the actual model weights being explained, illustrate that this risk is not merely theoretical.

The explanation fidelity testing methodology developed in Section 8.5 of this book exists specifically to guard against this failure mode, providing a concrete, repeatable test that an organization can run before trusting any specific explanation method's output, rather than assuming that a visually plausible attribution map is automatically a faithful one. Readers who take away only one methodological habit from this book should take away the discipline of testing explanation fidelity before relying on an explanation's content, a discipline that is unfortunately still inconsistently applied across the broader industry.

CHAPTER 3.

Literature Survey: Mapping the Explainability Landscape

Introduction

This chapter surveys the existing body of research on explainability for image-based deep learning in more depth than the historical sketch given in Chapter 2, organizing it around four threads: explainability for discriminative CNNs, interpretability for generative GANs, hybrid CNN-GAN architectures and their treatment of explainability, and the research gaps that motivate the framework developed in the remainder of this book.

The intent here is not encyclopedic coverage of every paper published on the topic, but a structured account of the major lines of work, organized so that a reader can see clearly where the field has built solid, reusable techniques, and where it has left open problems that practitioners building hybrid systems must currently solve on their own, often informally and without much guidance from the literature.

Structure

- Explainable AI in Discriminative Image Analytics
- Interpretability in Generative Models
- Hybrid CNN-GAN Architectures
- Research Gaps This Book Addresses

Explainable AI in Discriminative Image Analytics

Research on explainability for discriminative image models has, by a wide margin, the most mature literature of the four threads surveyed in this chapter. Early work concentrated on opening the black box of CNNs by visualizing their internal representations directly, examining learned filters and intermediate feature maps to understand what visual patterns each layer of the network had come to detect. Activation maximization techniques searched for, or synthesized, inputs that maximally excited individual neurons, building up an intuitive picture of the hierarchy from simple edge detectors in early layers to complex, semantically meaningful detectors in deeper layers.

Saliency-based and gradient-based approaches built on this foundation by connecting a model's output directly back to its input through the chain rule, producing pixel-level attribution maps that highlight which regions of a specific image contributed most to a specific prediction. These gradient methods evolved into a family of refinements addressing noise, saturation, and other artifacts of the basic gradient signal, and they remain among the most widely used explainability tools for CNNs precisely because they are computationally cheap and require no architectural changes to the underlying model.

Building on attribution, class-specific localization techniques offered both local and instance-scale understanding of model behavior, allowing practitioners to see not just that a model attended to a particular region, but what class that attention was supporting, which proved especially valuable for diagnosing misclassifications where a model attended to the right region but drew the wrong conclusion. Most recently, concept-based explanation methods have moved the field toward abstractions that map onto human semantic categories rather than raw pixels, attributing learned features to concepts that domain experts can recognize and reason about directly, considerably improving the practical trustworthiness of the resulting explanations.

Despite this progress, explainable image analytics research has, as a general pattern, remained focused almost entirely on discriminative models, leaving comparatively little guidance for practitioners who also need to explain the behavior of generative components in the same pipeline.

Interpretability in Generative Models

Interpretability research for GANs has developed along a substantially different and less mature path than its discriminative counterpart, in large part because the adversarial training dynamic and the high-dimensional latent space that GANs operate over do not lend themselves to the same gradient-attribution techniques that work well for classifiers. Unlike discriminative models, GANs lack an explicit decision space or a prediction to explain in the traditional sense, which means that interpretability research has had to invent its own vocabulary rather than borrowing directly from the CNN explainability toolkit.

The dominant line of existing work analyzes manipulations in the latent space, examining how systematic alterations to the latent variables fed into a generator change the semantic properties, shape, color, texture, of the resulting generated image. This has led naturally to research on disentangled representation learning, which aims to discover latent variables that each control a single, independent, and ideally human-interpretable factor of variation in the generated output, improving both the controllability and the interpretability of the generative process.

These approaches have produced genuine insight, but they tend to rely on largely qualitative judgments and heuristic estimation rather than the kind of standardized, quantitative metrics that discriminative explainability research has developed. The absence of standardized explainability metrics for generative models, and the corresponding absence of universal interpretability mechanisms comparable to gradient attribution for CNNs, limits the reproducibility, comparability, and reliability of GAN interpretability research, a limitation that becomes especially consequential in safety-critical or data-sensitive applications that rely on synthesis-based image generation.

Hybrid CNN-GAN Architectures

A separate and growing body of research has examined hybrid architectures that combine CNNs and GANs to take advantage of both paradigms within a single pipeline, applying these combinations to tasks such as data augmentation, semi-supervised learning, image reconstruction, and anomaly detection. In these approaches, CNNs are typically used to extract or discriminate features, while GANs are used to generate realistic synthetic samples that increase the diversity of training data or to identify outliers relative to a learned data distribution.

Performance results from this hybrid research direction have generally been encouraging, with measurable gains over either architecture used alone on a range of downstream tasks. However, explainability in these hybrid systems is, in the existing literature, treated largely as a secondary concern, addressed only incidentally if at all. The interaction between the discriminative and generative components introduces additional layers of complexity that further obscure an already opaque pair of architectures, and the result is that practitioners and end users of hybrid CNN-GAN systems are typically given little visibility into how synthesized data actually influences the decisions the system makes downstream, which in turn raises unresolved questions about accountability, the propagation of bias from synthetic data into model behavior, and the overall reliability of hybrid model outputs.

Research Gaps This Book Addresses

Synthesizing the three threads surveyed above reveals several specific and persistent gaps in the current state of explainable image analytics. First, explainability methods for GAN-based image synthesis remain comparatively scarce and largely qualitative, leaving practitioners with an incomplete understanding of the generative decision-making process relative to the much richer toolkit available for discriminative models. Second, unified explainable frameworks capable of addressing the interpretability of CNN-GAN hybrid architectures as a single coherent system, rather than as two separately explained components, are largely absent from the literature, even as hybrid architectures themselves become increasingly common in practice. Third, the lack of formal, standardized explainability metrics for generative models makes it difficult to benchmark different approaches objectively or to establish the kind of comparability that would let practitioners evaluate competing explainability techniques on equal footing.

These three gaps, taken together, define the problem this book sets out to solve. The framework introduced in the chapters that follow is constructed specifically to close them: it extends rigorous, quantitative explainability techniques to the GAN side of a hybrid pipeline rather than relying solely on qualitative latent-space exploration; it provides a unified aggregation and visualization layer that treats CNN and GAN explanations as components of one coherent explanatory account rather than two separate ones; and it introduces explicit, computable metrics for explainability that allow the framework's effectiveness to be measured and compared rather than asserted qualitatively.

The remaining chapters build this framework from the ground up, beginning with an architectural overview in Chapter 4 and proceeding through the mathematical formulations, implementation details, and experimental validation that establish the framework as a practical, deployable answer to the gaps identified in this chapter.

A Note on Reproducibility of the Comparative Survey Tables

The comparative tables presented earlier in this chapter summarize reported results from the cited literature rather than results independently reproduced by this book's author, and readers intending to use these tables as a basis for their own technical decisions should be aware of the limitations this distinction carries. Reported metrics in the explainability literature are computed under widely varying experimental conditions, varying datasets, varying model architectures, varying definitions of the same nominal metric, that make direct numerical comparison across rows of a summary table considerably less precise than the table's clean tabular presentation might suggest.

This book's own experimental results, presented beginning in Chapter 9, were independently reproduced under the controlled conditions described in that chapter's methodology section specifically so that the comparison between the proposed unified framework and the established CNN-only and GAN-only baselines would rest on a single consistent experimental protocol rather than on the heterogeneous reported figures discussed in this section. Readers who require apples-to-apples numerical comparison are encouraged to rely primarily on Chapter 9's controlled results and to treat this chapter's literature summary as a qualitative map of the field's conceptual landscape rather than as a precise quantitative benchmark.

How This Survey Was Conducted

The literature survey presented in this chapter draws on peer-reviewed publications in computer vision, machine learning, and human-computer interaction venues, supplemented by a smaller number of widely cited preprints and industry technical reports where they represent an influential or foundational contribution not yet captured in peer-reviewed form at the time of this book's writing. The survey deliberately prioritizes breadth of coverage across the discriminative, generative, and hybrid tracks discussed earlier in this chapter over exhaustive depth within any single track, consistent with this book's overall purpose of establishing a shared foundation for the unified framework introduced in Chapter 4 rather than producing a specialized review of any one narrow sub-literature.

Readers seeking a more exhaustive treatment of any single track surveyed in this chapter, the discriminative attribution literature specifically, for instance, are encouraged to consult the dedicated survey literature within that narrower field, several examples of which are cited in the reference list collected in Appendix A, rather than relying on this chapter's necessarily compressed treatment as a complete substitute for that more specialized literature.

Cross-Pollination Between Discriminative and Generative Explainability Research

While the literature surveyed in this chapter largely developed along separate discriminative and generative tracks, as discussed earlier, a smaller but increasingly visible body of research has begun explicitly cross-pollinating techniques between the two tracks, applying gradient-based attribution concepts originally developed for discriminative classifiers to questions about which input features most influence a generative model's output, and applying latent-space disentanglement concepts originally developed for generative models to questions about how a discriminative classifier's internal representation space is organized.

This cross-pollination is, in the authors' assessment, one of the more promising directions within the broader field, and the unified explainability layer presented in Chapter 7 can be understood as an applied, production-oriented instance of this same cross-pollination trend, translating concepts and validation techniques across the discriminative-generative boundary within a single operational framework rather than within a purely academic research exercise.

Positioning This Book's Contribution Within the Surveyed Field

Having surveyed the discriminative explainability literature, the generative interpretability literature, and the smaller hybrid literature combining both, it is useful to state directly where this book's own contribution, detailed across Chapters 4 through 9, is positioned relative to that survey. This book does not claim to introduce a fundamentally new attribution or interpretability algorithm; the gradient-based attribution, concept activation, and latent sensitivity techniques it builds on are drawn directly from the existing literature surveyed in this chapter.

The contribution this book makes is architectural and operational: a validated method for unifying these existing techniques into a single coherent framework spanning both discriminative and generative components, a formal metric for measuring the resulting framework's explainability quality in a way that supports meaningful comparison across deployments, and an operational treatment, covering production integration, governance, and case-study validation, that moves the underlying techniques from research demonstration toward production-ready engineering practice. Readers seeking novel underlying explanation algorithms should consult the primary research literature cited throughout this chapter; readers seeking a validated path to combining and operationalizing that existing research are the primary intended audience for the chapters that follow.

Methodological Approaches Across the Surveyed Literature

The explainability literature surveyed in this chapter divides along several methodological lines that are useful to make explicit before moving into this book's own framework in Chapter 4. One line separates gradient-based methods, which compute an explanation by examining how the model's output changes with respect to small changes in its input or internal activations, from perturbation-based methods, which compute an explanation by directly modifying or occluding parts of the input and observing the resulting change in output, without requiring access to internal gradients at all.

A second line separates methods that produce a single, model-specific explanation tailored to the exact architecture being explained from model-agnostic methods designed to treat the underlying model as a black box and explain any model regardless of its internal structure, typically by fitting a simpler, locally interpretable surrogate model around the prediction of interest. Model-specific gradient methods generally offer better computational efficiency and tighter fidelity to the actual model computation, at the cost of requiring architecture-specific implementation; model-agnostic methods offer broader applicability at some cost to both speed and, in several documented cases, fidelity.

The framework presented in this book, consistent with the gaps identified later in this chapter, adopts model-specific gradient-based methods as its primary mechanism for the CNN module, described fully in Chapter 5, on the grounds that the efficiency and fidelity advantages of model-specific approaches outweigh the generality advantages of model-agnostic alternatives for the production deployment scenarios this book is primarily concerned with.

Evaluation Practices in Prior Work

A recurring methodological weakness across much of the surveyed literature, and one of the research gaps formalized later in this chapter, concerns how explanation quality has historically been evaluated. A substantial portion of published explainability research relies primarily on qualitative visual inspection, presenting a small number of example attribution maps or generated visualizations and asking the reader to judge, by eye, whether the explanation appears reasonable. This evaluation approach is intuitive and easy to communicate, but it does not scale to systematic validation across a large population of predictions, and it is vulnerable to selection bias in which examples are chosen for the figure.

A smaller but growing portion of the literature has adopted more rigorous quantitative evaluation, including sanity checks that test whether an attribution method's output changes appropriately when the underlying model's weights are randomized or retrained, and localization-based metrics that test whether an attribution map's highlighted regions align with independently annotated ground-truth regions of interest. These quantitative approaches are more labor-intensive to implement but provide a far more defensible basis for claiming that an explanation method is actually faithful to model behavior, and they directly inform the explanation fidelity methodology this book formalizes in Section 8.5.

CHAPTER 4.

Framework Overview: A Unified Explainable CNN-GAN Architecture

Introduction

This chapter introduces the explainable AI framework that is the central technical contribution of this book, originally proposed in the author's peer-reviewed paper on explainable image analytics and synthetic image creation. Where the original paper presented the framework in condensed form appropriate to a conference-length submission, this chapter and the two that follow it unpack each module in considerably more depth, with the mathematical grounding, design rationale, and implementation guidance that a practitioner needs to actually build the system rather than merely read about it.

The framework rests on a simple organizing idea: rather than treating CNN explainability and GAN explainability as separate problems requiring separate tooling, it defines three tightly coupled modules that share a common explanatory vocabulary, so that the output of one module can be meaningfully compared with, and combined with, the output of another.

Structure

- Design Principles Behind the Framework
- The Three Core Modules
- Data Flow Through the Framework
- Where the Framework Sits in a Production Pipeline

Design Principles Behind the Framework

Three design principles guided the construction of this framework, and understanding them up front makes the architectural decisions in the rest of this chapter considerably easier to follow.

The first principle is non-invasiveness. The framework is designed to attach to an already-trained CNN and an already-trained GAN without requiring either to be retrained or architecturally modified. This matters enormously in practice, because most organizations adopting an explainability layer are doing so on top of existing production models that represent a substantial prior investment in training time, data curation, and validation. A framework that demanded retraining from scratch would face an adoption barrier high enough to make it impractical for most real deployments.

The second principle is modular coupling. The CNN explainability module and the GAN explainability module are each independently useful and can, in principle, be deployed without the other. But they are designed from the outset to plug into a shared aggregation layer, so that an organization running only a CNN classifier today can add a GAN component later without redesigning its explainability tooling, and vice versa.

The third principle is metric-first design. Every explanation the framework produces, whether a saliency map, a concept score, or a latent sensitivity profile, is backed by an explicit, computable metric rather than a purely qualitative visualization. This is what allows the framework's explainability score, introduced in Chapter 8, to be reported as a single number alongside accuracy and generative fidelity metrics, making explainability a first-class, measurable property of the system rather than a vague claim.

The Three Core Modules

The framework consists of three modules, each addressed in detail in this chapter and the two that follow.

The first module, Explainable CNN-Based Image Analytics, is responsible for discriminative tasks: classification, detection, or feature extraction performed by a convolutional network. This module is enhanced with both post-hoc explanation methods, principally gradient-based attribution, and feature-level explanation methods, principally Concept Activation Vectors, so that the regions and semantic concepts the model relies upon are surfaced alongside every prediction.

The second module, Explainable GAN-Based Synthetic Image Generation, is responsible for generative tasks: producing realistic synthetic images for data augmentation, anomaly modeling, or other downstream uses. This module is made explainable through latent space sensitivity analysis, which quantifies how strongly each dimension of the generator's input latent vector influences the visual properties of the output image, giving practitioners a controllable, semantically grounded way to understand and manipulate the generation process.

The third module, the Unified Explanation Aggregation and Visualization Layer, is the architectural innovation that distinguishes this framework from prior work that treats

CNN and GAN explainability separately. This layer normalizes the outputs of the first two modules onto a common scale, aligns them so they can be visualized side by side, and produces consolidated reports that let a single stakeholder reason about the entire pipeline's behavior, discriminative and generative, in one coherent view.

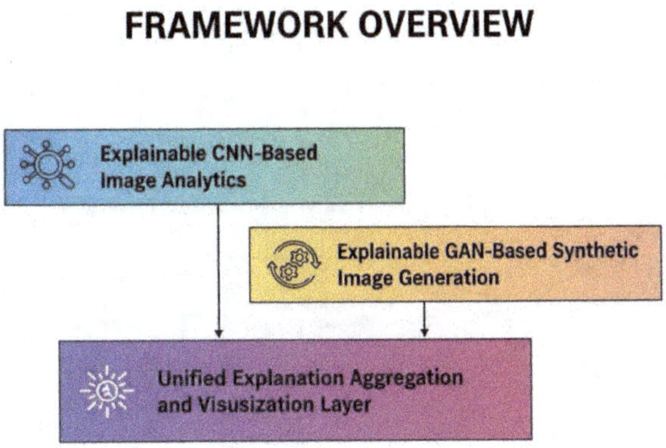

Figure 4.1: High-level overview of the proposed framework, showing the explainable CNN module and explainable GAN module feeding into the unified explanation aggregation and visualization layer.

Data Flow Through the Framework

To make the architecture concrete, it helps to trace a single image through the framework end to end. An input image enters the CNN module, which produces both a class prediction and, alongside it, a gradient-based attribution map and a set of concept relevance scores describing which learned concepts most strongly supported the prediction. Separately, if the system also includes a generative component, a latent vector enters the GAN module, which produces a synthetic image along with a latent sensitivity profile describing how each latent dimension influenced the visual characteristics of that output.

Both sets of outputs, the CNN's attribution and concept scores and the GAN's latent sensitivity profile, are passed to the unified aggregation layer. There, they are normalized onto comparable scales, typically by converting raw attribution magnitudes and sensitivity values into bounded relevance scores, and then rendered into a combined visualization that places the original image, its attribution map, any relevant synthetic comparison image, and a small set of summary statistics into a single composite view.

This combined view is what gets surfaced to the end user or auditor, rather than two disconnected sets of diagnostic output from two unrelated tools. The practical effect is that a practitioner investigating, say, a misclassification that occurred shortly after a batch of synthetic training images was introduced can examine both the CNN's attribution pattern on the misclassified instance and the latent sensitivity profile of the synthetic images that may have influenced training, within the same interface and using the same scoring conventions.

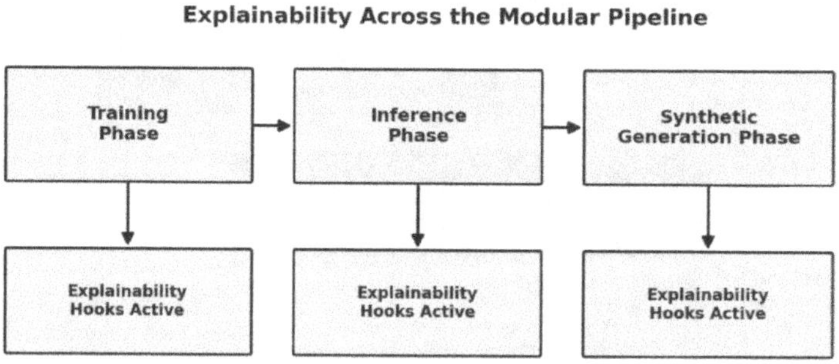

Figure 4.2: Explainability hooks remain active across the training, inference, and synthetic generation phases of the modular pipeline.

Where the Framework Sits in a Production Pipeline

The framework is designed to be inserted at three points in a typical production machine learning pipeline. During training, explainability hooks can be attached to periodically sample concept activation scores and latent sensitivity profiles, building up a baseline understanding of model behavior before deployment. During inference, the CNN attribution and concept-scoring components run alongside every prediction, at a computational cost designed to remain small relative to the forward pass itself. During synthetic generation, the GAN's latent sensitivity analysis can be run either online, attached to every generation request, or offline, as a periodic audit of the generator's behavior across a sample of the latent space.

This three-point integration is deliberately flexible. Organizations with strict latency requirements on the inference path can choose to run the heavier explainability computations offline or asynchronously, producing explanations that lag the prediction itself by seconds or minutes rather than blocking it. Organizations operating in more strictly regulated environments, where every decision must be explainable at the moment it is made, can choose to run the full explainability stack synchronously, accepting the additional latency in exchange for an explanation that accompanies every output. The framework's modularity is what makes this kind of deployment-specific tuning possible without redesigning the underlying explainability logic.

Why the Three Modules Are Presented Sequentially Rather Than Jointly

This book introduces the explainable CNN module, the explainable GAN module, and the unified explanation layer sequentially across Chapters 5 through 7, even though the proposed framework treats all three as a single integrated system once deployed. This sequential presentation reflects a pedagogical choice rather than an architectural one: each module's internal mechanics are sufficiently involved that introducing all three simultaneously would force the reader to track three sets of unfamiliar mathematical notation at once, substantially raising the cognitive burden of the early chapters without a corresponding gain in comprehension.

Readers who already possess working familiarity with gradient-based attribution methods and concept activation vectors from prior exposure to the discriminative explainability literature may reasonably choose to skim Chapter 5 and proceed directly to Chapter 6; readers arriving with the opposite background may follow the same logic in reverse. Chapter 7's unified explanation layer, however, depends on notation and intuitions established in both preceding chapters and is not recommended as a skip-ahead destination regardless of the reader's prior background, since its core contribution is precisely the reconciliation of the two preceding modules' otherwise incompatible explanation outputs.

A Reference Implementation Checklist

Organizations beginning an implementation of the framework described in this chapter and elaborated across Chapters 5 through 8 often find it useful to work from a concrete checklist rather than from the architectural description alone. At minimum, a viable initial implementation requires a differentiable discriminative model exposing access to intermediate-layer activations for the gradient-based attribution and concept activation methods described in Chapter 5, a generative model exposing direct access to its latent input vector for the sensitivity analysis described in Chapter 6, a defined and validated concept vocabulary appropriate to the deployment domain, and a configured weighting scheme for the unified layer's aggregation logic described in Chapter 7.

Beyond these minimum technical prerequisites, a successful implementation additionally requires the organizational commitments discussed in Chapter 12, an established governance review with real enforcement authority and a documented audit trail process, before the framework's output can be meaningfully relied upon in a production decision-making context rather than treated as a research prototype generating explanations no governance process actually consumes.

Versioning the Framework Itself

Beyond the model versioning discipline discussed in Chapter 10, organizations adopting this framework should also version the framework's own configuration, the specific concept vocabulary in use, the perturbation magnitudes used in latent sensitivity analysis, the weighting scheme used in the unified layer's aggregation logic, as a distinct artifact from the underlying CNN and GAN model versions. A change to the concept vocabulary, for instance adding a newly curated domain-specific concept following the curation process described in Chapter 5, can materially change the unified explainability score reported for an otherwise unchanged underlying model, and an audit trail that tracks only model versions without also tracking framework configuration versions will be unable to distinguish a genuine change in model behavior from a change in how that behavior is being measured.

This framework-level versioning need not be elaborate; a simple, append-only log recording each configuration change alongside its effective date and the rationale for the change is typically sufficient, provided that log is actually consulted during the periodic governance self-audit discussed in Chapter 12 rather than maintained purely as an unused formality.

Extending the Framework to New Modalities

The three-module architecture described in this chapter was designed around the specific combination of CNN-based discriminative analytics and GAN-based generative synthesis that forms this book's primary subject, but the design's narrow interface contracts, discussed earlier, are intended to support extension to adjacent modalities without a full architectural redesign. An organization wishing to extend the framework to cover video rather than static images, for instance, would need to extend the explainable CNN module's attribution computation to account for the temporal dimension, but could in principle leave the unified layer's aggregation and auditing logic largely unchanged, since that logic operates on the normalized, modality-agnostic explanation signals the lower-level modules expose rather than on raw video or image data directly.

This extensibility remains, at the time of this book's writing, more a design intention validated through architectural analysis than an extension that has been fully implemented and field-tested in the way the core CNN-GAN framework has been across the case studies in Chapter 11, and organizations attempting such an extension should expect to encounter modality-specific challenges that this book, focused on the static image case, does not directly address.

Design Trade-offs Considered and Rejected

Before settling on the three-module architecture described earlier in this chapter, several alternative designs were considered and ultimately rejected, and reviewing them clarifies why the adopted structure takes the shape it does. A fully monolithic design, in which a single explainability subsystem operated directly on both the CNN and GAN components without a clear modular boundary, was rejected because it could not be cleanly extended to new generative architectures, such as the diffusion-based models discussed in Chapter 13, without rewriting the explanation logic for the discriminative half of the system as a side effect.

A fully decoupled design, in which CNN and GAN explainability were treated as entirely separate subsystems with no shared aggregation layer, was rejected for the opposite reason: it left no mechanism for the cross-component bias auditing described in Chapter 7, in which a synthetic image generated by the GAN module and subsequently misclassified by the CNN module needs to be traced back through both components to determine where in the pipeline a systematic bias originated. The three-module design adopted in this book represents a deliberate middle position, preserving independent extensibility for each generative or discriminative component while still providing the shared aggregation layer that cross-component analysis requires.

A third alternative, building explainability directly into the model architecture itself, for example by constraining the CNN to use only interpretable building blocks from the outset rather than applying post-hoc attribution to an otherwise standard architecture, was rejected on practical grounds: it would have required organizations adopting the framework to retrain or replace existing production models rather than instrument them, a substantially higher adoption cost that the post-hoc design explicitly avoids.

Interface Contracts Between Modules

The three-module architecture depends on well-defined interface contracts between modules to remain maintainable as each module evolves independently. The explainable CNN module, described fully in Chapter 5, exposes a contract consisting of a per-prediction attribution map at the same spatial resolution as the input image, a set of concept activation scores keyed to a configurable concept vocabulary, and a confidence-weighted summary suitable for the unified layer's aggregation logic. The explainable GAN module, described fully in Chapter 6, exposes an analogous contract consisting of a per-dimension latent sensitivity profile, a set of identified semantically meaningful latent directions, and a generation-quality flag indicating whether a given synthetic sample fell within or outside the distribution of training-time generation quality.

These contracts are intentionally narrow, exposing only the information the unified layer actually needs to perform normalization, alignment, and aggregation, rather than exposing each module's full internal state. This narrowness is a direct consequence of the lesson drawn from the design trade-offs discussed earlier: a narrow, stable interface allows the internal implementation of either module, including a future replacement of the GAN module's generative backbone with a diffusion-based architecture, to evolve without requiring changes to the unified layer or to any downstream governance and documentation processes built on top of it.

CHAPTER 5.

The Explainable CNN Module

Introduction

This chapter develops the first of the framework's three modules in full mathematical and practical detail: the explainable CNN architecture responsible for discriminative image analytics. The module is built around two complementary explanation mechanisms, gradient-based attribution for instance-level, pixel-grounded explanations, and Concept Activation Vectors for feature-level, semantically grounded explanations. Used together, these two mechanisms give a practitioner both a fine-grained visual account of a single prediction and an abstract, human-readable account of which general concepts the model relies upon across many predictions.

Structure

- Setting Up the Discriminative Task
- Gradient-Based Attribution: Mathematical Formulation
- Producing and Reading Attribution Maps
- Concept Activation Vectors: From Pixels to Semantics
- The TCAV Score and Its Interpretation
- Combining Attribution and Concepts in Practice

Setting Up the Discriminative Task

The explainable CNN module begins with the standard discriminative setup: an input image is represented as a three-dimensional tensor with a height, width, and a number of channels corresponding to spatial resolution and color information. The convolutional network is trained to map this tensor to a class label drawn from a fixed set of target classes, learning, through successive layers of feature extraction, a hierarchy that progresses from low-level patterns such as edges and textures to high-level semantic concepts that support the final classification decision.

This mapping from image to label is the ordinary discriminative use of a CNN, and nothing about the architecture itself needs to change to make it explainable. What changes is the addition of two analysis mechanisms that operate on top of the trained network: gradient-based attribution, which explains individual predictions, and concept-based interpretability, which explains the network's general reliance on human-meaningful visual concepts.

Gradient-Based Attribution: Mathematical Formulation

Gradient-based attribution works by computing the sensitivity of a model's output score for a particular class with respect to the input image. Concretely, given an input image and a class of interest, the attribution method computes the gradient of the predicted class score with respect to each pixel of the input. This gradient is, intuitively, a measure of how much a small change to a given pixel would change the model's confidence in that class: pixels with a large-magnitude gradient are pixels the model is most sensitive to, and are therefore strong candidates for having driven the prediction.

Formally, let the network's output for class c, given input image x, be denoted as a scalar score Sc(x). The raw attribution for the input is the gradient of this score with respect to the input, taken pixel by pixel. Because this gradient can be positive or negative depending on whether increasing a pixel's intensity would increase or decrease the class score, attribution methods typically take the absolute value or otherwise rectify the gradient before visualization, so that the resulting map highlights regions of influence regardless of the direction of that influence.

The resulting attribution map has the same spatial dimensions as the input image, with each entry representing the relative importance of the corresponding pixel to the predicted class. This is what allows the attribution map to be rendered as a heatmap overlay directly on top of the original image, giving an immediately interpretable visual account of where the network was looking when it made its decision.

Producing and Reading Attribution Maps

In practice, raw gradients are often noisy, with attribution scattered across many pixels in a way that does not cleanly correspond to a single coherent region. Several refinements address this. Smoothing the gradient by averaging over many small perturbations of the input reduces pixel-level noise while preserving the overall shape of the attribution. Integrating the gradient along a path from a neutral baseline image to the actual input addresses a different failure mode, where the raw gradient can underestimate the importance of features that the network's response has effectively saturated against.

Reading an attribution map well requires some practiced judgment. A map that concentrates tightly on the semantically relevant object, a tumor in a medical scan, a defect in an industrial part, is a strong positive signal that the model has learned the intended task. A map that instead lights up on background regions, watermarks, or other spurious artifacts is a warning sign of a model that has learned a shortcut correlated with the label in the training data but not causally related to the actual visual concept the label is meant to capture. This kind of diagnostic use of attribution maps, looking not just at whether the prediction is correct but at whether the reasoning behind it is sound, is one of the most operationally valuable applications of gradient-based attribution.

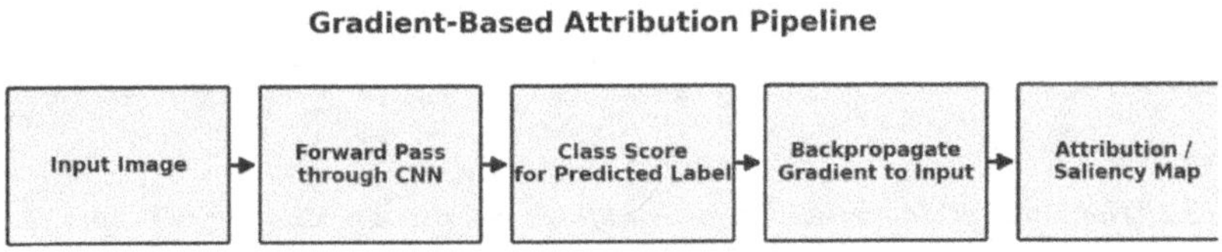

***Figure 5.1:** The gradient-based attribution pipeline: from input image, through the forward pass and class score, to a backpropagated attribution map.*

Concept Activation Vectors: From Pixels to Semantics

Pixel-level attribution is faithful and precise, but it does not, by itself, tell a practitioner whether the model's reliance on a region corresponds to a meaningful semantic concept or an arbitrary pattern. Concept Activation Vectors address this gap by asking a more abstract question: does a human-defined concept, such as stripes, fur, wheels, or any other visual property a domain expert cares about, correspond to a coherent direction in the network's internal feature space, and if so, how strongly does that direction influence the model's confidence in a particular class?

Constructing a Concept Activation Vector begins with two sets of example images: a positive set containing clear examples of the concept of interest, and a negative or random set that does not contain the concept. Both sets of images are passed through the network up to a chosen internal layer, producing a set of activation vectors for each example. A linear classifier is then trained to separate the positive examples' activations from the negative examples' activations in that layer's feature space. The direction defined by this linear classifier, orthogonal to its decision boundary, is the Concept Activation Vector: a direction in the network's internal representation that corresponds to the presence or absence of the target concept.

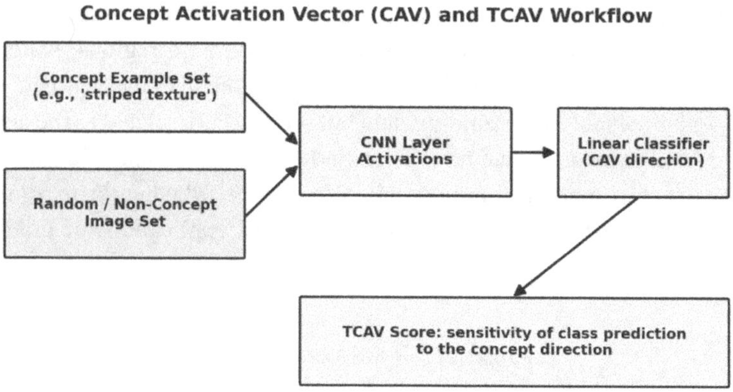

Figure 5.2: The Concept Activation Vector workflow: positive and negative concept example sets are passed through a CNN layer, and a linear classifier defines the CAV direction used to compute a TCAV score.

The TCAV Score and Its Interpretation

Once a Concept Activation Vector has been constructed, the framework computes a Testing with Concept Activation Vectors score, or TCAV score, which measures how often the model's prediction for a given class would be pushed in a positive direction by moving the relevant layer's activation slightly along the concept direction, across a sample of images from that class. A high TCAV score for a concept and class pair indicates that the model's confidence in that class systematically increases as the presence of that concept increases, in a way that is statistically distinguishable from what would happen with a random direction in the same feature space.

TCAV scores are valuable precisely because they let a domain expert ask targeted, hypothesis-driven questions about a model's behavior. A radiologist might ask whether a model's confidence in a particular diagnosis is driven by a concept like irregular border texture, a question that a TCAV score can answer directly and quantitatively, in a way that a raw attribution map, however precise, cannot, because attribution maps describe where the model is looking but not what semantic property of that region matters to the prediction.

Used together, gradient-based attribution and Concept Activation Vectors give the explainable CNN module a layered explanatory capability: attribution maps answer the question of where, for a single instance, and TCAV scores answer the question of what concept, across many instances. The combination considerably strengthens the practical interpretability of the module compared to either technique used in isolation.

Combining Attribution and Concepts in Practice

In a deployed system, the two explanation mechanisms are typically surfaced together rather than separately. A practitioner reviewing a single prediction sees the attribution map overlaid on the input image, alongside a short list of the concepts with the highest TCAV scores for the predicted class, computed once during a model validation pass and cached for efficient lookup at inference time. This combination lets a stakeholder move fluidly between an instance-specific visual account and a more general, semantically grounded account of what the model tends to rely on.

This same combination is also what feeds the unified aggregation layer described in Chapter 4 and developed further in Chapter 7. The attribution map and the concept relevance scores produced by this module are normalized onto the framework's common explanatory scale, allowing them to be directly compared against the latent sensitivity outputs of the GAN module covered in the next chapter, and ultimately rolled up into the single explainability score reported alongside accuracy and generative fidelity in the experimental results of Chapter 8.

Failure Modes of Gradient-Based Attribution Worth Naming Explicitly

The gradient-based attribution methods introduced in this chapter are powerful but not infallible, and a responsible treatment of explainable CNN architectures requires naming their failure modes explicitly rather than presenting them as a uniformly reliable solution to the black-box problem. Gradient saturation, in which a neuron's activation function operates in a flat region of its response curve for a given input, can cause attribution methods that rely directly on the raw gradient to substantially underweight pixels that the model nonetheless used heavily in reaching its decision, since the local gradient at a saturated activation approaches zero regardless of the activation's actual causal importance to the downstream decision.

Adversarial fragility represents a related but distinct failure mode: small, often visually imperceptible perturbations to an input image can produce a dramatically different attribution map even when the model's classification output is unchanged, undermining the intuitive expectation that similar inputs producing similar outputs ought to receive similar explanations. The concept activation vector approach introduced later in this chapter partially mitigates both failure modes by operating at the level of learned semantic concepts rather than raw pixel gradients, though it introduces its own dependency on concept vocabulary completeness discussed in Section 5.6. A practitioner deploying this book's framework in a high-stakes setting should treat attribution-based explanations as one evidentiary signal among several rather than as a sufficient explanation on their own, a theme this book returns to directly in Chapter 7's discussion of multi-signal reconciliation.

Transferability of Attribution Methods Across Trained Models

A question that arises naturally once an organization has validated the explainable CNN module against one trained model is whether that validation transfers to a subsequent model trained on similar data with a similar architecture but different weights, for instance a routine retraining cycle that updates a production classifier on newly collected data without changing its underlying architecture. The explanation fidelity testing methodology introduced in Section 8.5 does not transfer automatically across such a retraining event, because attribution stability is a property of the specific trained weights being explained, not of the architecture in the abstract, and a retrained model with substantially different weights can exhibit meaningfully different attribution stability even when its raw classification accuracy remains essentially unchanged.

Organizations operating the framework in production should therefore treat explanation fidelity validation as a required step in every model retraining cycle, not only in the initial deployment, a requirement that the versioning and documentation discipline described in Chapter 10 and Chapter 12 is specifically designed to enforce systematically rather than leaving to ad hoc judgment at each retraining event.

Attribution at Scale: Batch Processing Considerations

The attribution computation described earlier in this chapter is straightforward to apply to a single image but requires additional engineering care when applied across the large batches of images typical of the population-level auditing use case described in Chapter 7. Computing per-image gradient-based attribution for a population of tens of thousands of images, the scale typically required for the kind of bias audit discussed in Chapter 12, multiplies the per-image computational cost discussed in Chapter 10 by a correspondingly large factor, and naive batch implementations that simply loop over images one at a time often fail to fully utilize available GPU parallelism.

Production implementations of the explainable CNN module should batch the gradient computation itself, processing many images through a single forward and backward pass rather than issuing one pass per image, an optimization that is conceptually straightforward but requires careful attention to how class-discriminative attribution methods select which output class's gradient to propagate when different images in the batch belong to different predicted classes, a detail that is easy to implement incorrectly and that should be specifically validated during the explanation fidelity testing described in Section 8.5 before relying on batch-computed attribution for production-scale auditing.

Attribution and Adversarial Robustness

A connection worth making explicit, since it bears on how attribution results should be interpreted in security-sensitive deployments such as the surveillance case study discussed in Chapter 11, concerns the relationship between attribution stability and adversarial robustness. Models that are more robust to adversarial perturbations, small, deliberately crafted input modifications designed to cause misclassification, tend empirically to produce more stable, less noisy attribution maps than models that are highly vulnerable to such perturbations, a pattern consistent with the intuition that adversarial vulnerability and attribution instability both reflect a model relying on narrow, brittle decision boundaries rather than broad, well-generalized ones.

This relationship suggests a secondary, diagnostic use for the attribution stability component of the explanation fidelity testing described in Section 8.5: a model exhibiting poor attribution stability under the fidelity test may also be unusually vulnerable to adversarial manipulation, a possibility that security-conscious deployments should investigate directly using dedicated adversarial robustness testing rather than relying on attribution stability as a substitute for that more specialized evaluation.

Choosing Among Competing Attribution Methods

The gradient-based attribution literature surveyed in Chapter 3 offers several specific techniques beyond the basic saliency map computation introduced earlier in this chapter, and a practical implementation of the explainable CNN module must choose among them. Methods that propagate gradients through a guided or rectified backward pass tend to produce visually sharper, more localized attribution maps than the raw gradient computation, at some cost to the formal interpretability of exactly what the resulting map represents mathematically. Methods that aggregate gradient information at intermediate convolutional layers rather than at the input pixel layer tend to produce coarser but often more semantically coherent regions of interest, since intermediate layers in a trained CNN typically encode object-part or texture-level representations rather than raw pixel intensities.

The framework presented in this book defaults to a class-discriminative, intermediate-layer gradient method for the primary attribution map, on the grounds that the resulting coarser, more semantically coherent regions tend to align better with the stakeholder-relative explanation goals discussed in Chapter 2, while retaining the option to compute finer-grained, pixel-level attribution as a supplementary signal when the deployment context, such as the precise lesion boundary delineation required in the medical imaging case study of Chapter 11, specifically calls for it.

Building and Validating a Concept Vocabulary

The concept activation vector technique introduced earlier in this chapter depends entirely on the quality of the concept vocabulary used to define each concept, a curated set of example images representing the concept of interest alongside a contrasting set of random or negative examples. A poorly curated concept set, one that inadvertently bundles the concept of interest together with an unrelated but visually correlated attribute, will produce a concept activation vector that scores the unrelated attribute rather than the intended concept, a failure mode that is easy to introduce inadvertently and difficult to detect without deliberate validation.

This book recommends a validation step, beyond the basic linear classifier training described earlier, in which the candidate concept activation vector is tested against a held-out set of example images known to contain or lack the concept, confirming that the vector's score reliably separates these held-out examples before the vector is accepted into the production concept vocabulary. Organizations curating domain-specific concept vocabularies, an extension discussed further in Chapter 13, should treat this validation step as mandatory rather than optional, since the downstream trust that domain experts place in concept-based explanations depends directly on the rigor applied during this curation phase.

Common Failure Modes in CNN Attribution

Several failure modes recur often enough in practical deployments of CNN attribution methods to warrant explicit discussion. The first, attribution diffusion, occurs when a model's decision genuinely depends on a broad, spatially distributed pattern rather than a small, localized region, producing an attribution map that is technically faithful but visually unsatisfying because it does not point to a single, easily described region of interest; this is not a flaw in the attribution method but a faithful reflection of how the underlying model actually reasons, and it should not be mistaken for an attribution failure.

The second, background leakage, occurs when an attribution map highlights regions outside the object of interest, frequently because the model has learned a spurious correlation between the background context and the target class during training, a pattern that attribution genuinely and usefully surfaces rather than obscures, since it identifies a real weakness in the underlying model rather than a weakness in the explanation method. The third, attribution instability under near-imperceptible input perturbation, is the failure mode the explanation fidelity testing described in Section 8.5 is specifically designed to detect, and any attribution method exhibiting substantial instability under such perturbation should be treated with caution regardless of how visually compelling its output appears on any individual example.

CHAPTER 6.

The Explainable GAN Module

Introduction

This chapter develops the second of the framework's three modules: the explainable GAN architecture responsible for synthetic image generation. Where the explainable CNN module of Chapter 5 anchors its explanations to a discrete prediction, the explainable GAN module has no such anchor to work with. Its explanations instead center on the structure of the generator's latent space, asking which dimensions of that space control which visual properties of the output, and how sensitive the generation process is to small perturbations along each dimension.

Structure

- The Adversarial Training Objective, Revisited
- Why GANs Resist Conventional Attribution
- Latent Space Sensitivity Analysis: Mathematical Formulation
- Disentanglement and Semantic Control
- Practical Considerations in Latent Sensitivity Analysis
- What the GAN Module Delivers to the Unified Layer

The Adversarial Training Objective, Revisited

A Generative Adversarial Network consists of two networks trained in opposition. The generator takes a latent vector drawn from a fixed, simple distribution, typically a standard normal or uniform distribution, and maps it to a synthetic image. The discriminator takes an image, either a real one drawn from the training set or a synthetic one produced by the generator, and outputs a probability that the image is real. The generator is trained to maximize the discriminator's confusion, while the discriminator is trained to maximize its own ability to tell real from synthetic images apart.

This adversarial pressure is what drives the generator toward producing increasingly realistic images over the course of training: any systematic flaw in the generator's output that the discriminator learns to detect becomes a training signal pushing the generator to correct that flaw. The training process can be understood as a minimax game, in which the discriminator's objective is maximized with respect to its own parameters while the generator's objective is minimized with respect to its parameters, with each network's updates depending on the current state of the other.

Why GANs Resist Conventional Attribution

The gradient-based attribution technique described in Chapter 5 relies on a specific structural feature of the discriminative setting: there is a class score, a single scalar output, whose sensitivity to the input can be computed and visualized. A GAN's generator has no equivalent scalar output to anchor an attribution computation to. Its output is an entire image, not a single class score, and there is no natural notion of which pixel of a multi-dimensional output a given input dimension is most responsible for in the same way that attribution methods describe which input pixel a class score is most sensitive to.

This structural mismatch is why GAN interpretability research, as surveyed in Chapter 3, has developed its own distinct toolkit centered on the latent space rather than on attribution in the discriminative sense. The explainable GAN module in this framework follows that tradition, building its explanations around the sensitivity of the generated image to each dimension of the latent input vector, rather than attempting to force the generator into an attribution framework that does not naturally fit its structure.

Latent Space Sensitivity Analysis: Mathematical Formulation

Latent space sensitivity analysis treats each dimension of the generator's latent input vector as a potential semantic control and measures how much perturbing that single dimension changes the generated output. Concretely, given a baseline latent vector z and a small perturbation delta applied to a single dimension i, the generator produces two images: one from the unperturbed vector z, and one from the perturbed vector z with the i-th dimension shifted by delta. The sensitivity of the generated image to dimension i is then quantified by measuring the difference between these two output images, using an image-level distance or similarity metric appropriate to the visual properties under consideration.

Repeating this perturbation across many dimensions, and across many baseline latent vectors sampled from the latent distribution, produces a sensitivity profile: a score for each latent dimension indicating, on average, how strongly that dimension influences the visual characteristics of the generated output. Dimensions with high sensitivity scores are strong candidates for controlling salient, perceptible visual properties of the image, such as overall shape, dominant color, or coarse structural layout, while dimensions with low sensitivity scores typically contribute only fine-grained or perceptually subtle variation.

This sensitivity profile is the GAN module's principal explanatory output, and it plays the same structural role for the GAN that the attribution map plays for the CNN: it is a quantitative, per-dimension account of which parts of the model's input are responsible for which parts of its behavior, expressed in a form that can be visualized, compared across models, and fed into the unified aggregation layer described in the next chapter.

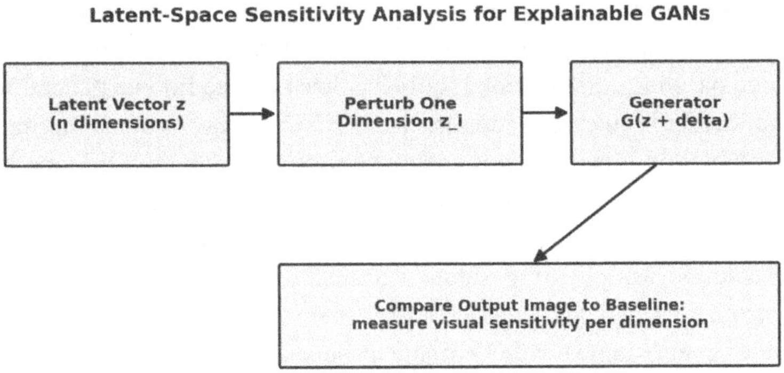

Figure 6.1: Latent-space sensitivity analysis: perturbing a single dimension of the latent vector and comparing the resulting generated image against the baseline output.

Disentanglement and Semantic Control

A latent space is described as well-disentangled when individual dimensions, or small, well-defined groups of dimensions, each control a single, semantically coherent factor of variation in the generated output, such as pose, lighting, or object scale, with minimal interference between dimensions. Disentanglement is valuable for explainability because it lets a sensitivity score on a given dimension be mapped onto a human-recognizable label, turning a purely numerical sensitivity profile into a semantic account of the generator's behavior: this dimension controls brightness, that one controls orientation, and so on.

In practice, the degree of disentanglement varies considerably depending on how the GAN was trained, and few production generators achieve perfect disentanglement without specialized training objectives designed explicitly to encourage it. The explainable GAN module in this framework does not assume perfect disentanglement; instead, it reports sensitivity scores honestly even when a dimension appears to influence multiple visual properties simultaneously, and it flags dimensions whose effects are difficult to characterize cleanly as a signal that the latent space, for that model, has not been learned in a maximally interpretable way. This honesty is important: a framework that artificially forced a clean semantic label onto every latent dimension would produce explanations that look more confident than the underlying model actually supports.

Practical Considerations in Latent Sensitivity Analysis

Running a full sensitivity analysis across every dimension of a high-dimensional latent space, for many baseline vectors, can be computationally expensive, since each dimension and baseline combination requires at least one additional generator forward pass. In practice, the framework supports several strategies for managing this cost. A coarse, low-resolution sensitivity sweep can be run first to identify the small subset of dimensions with non-trivial sensitivity scores, after which a more detailed analysis is concentrated only on that subset. Alternatively, sensitivity analysis can be run offline, on a representative sample of baseline vectors, with the resulting per-dimension sensitivity profile cached and reused across many generation requests rather than recomputed for every single synthetic image produced in production.

The choice between these strategies depends on how the generative component is being used. A system that generates synthetic images for periodic, offline data augmentation can afford a thorough, infrequent sensitivity analysis. A system that generates images interactively, in response to user-specified parameters, may need a faster, cached sensitivity profile that trades some precision for the responsiveness an interactive use case requires.

What the GAN Module Delivers to the Unified Layer

The explainable GAN module's output, the per-dimension latent sensitivity profile and, where available, semantic labels for well-disentangled dimensions, is passed forward to the unified aggregation layer in the same way the CNN module's attribution maps and concept scores are. The aggregation layer normalizes the GAN's sensitivity scores onto the same bounded scale used for the CNN's attribution and concept relevance scores, which is what allows the two modules' outputs to be visualized side by side and combined into the single explainability score discussed in Chapter 8.

This normalization step is not merely cosmetic. It is the technical mechanism that allows the framework to treat discriminative and generative explainability as a single coherent problem rather than two separate ones, and it is described in full in the next chapter, which is devoted entirely to the design and operation of the unified explainability layer.

Mode Collapse as an Explainability Problem, Not Only a Quality Problem

Mode collapse, the well-documented tendency of adversarially trained generators to produce a narrower diversity of outputs than the true data distribution contains, is typically discussed in the GAN literature purely as a generative quality problem, measured through diversity metrics and addressed through training-time interventions such as minibatch discrimination or unrolled optimization. This book's explainable GAN module reframes mode collapse as additionally an explainability problem deserving its own diagnostic treatment, since a generator exhibiting partial mode collapse will produce latent-space sensitivity explanations, of the kind introduced earlier in this chapter, that systematically understate the true sensitivity of the underlying data distribution to certain latent directions simply because the collapsed generator has stopped exploring those directions at all.

Practically, this means a latent sensitivity analysis performed on a generator suffering from undiagnosed mode collapse may report a misleadingly narrow set of semantically meaningful latent directions, creating a false impression of a simpler, more interpretable latent space than the generator actually possesses once collapse is corrected through retraining. Section 6.7 introduces a lightweight diagnostic, comparing latent sensitivity explanations before and after a targeted diversity-promoting fine-tuning pass, that allows a practitioner to distinguish a genuinely simple latent space from one whose apparent simplicity is an artifact of incomplete mode coverage.

Comparing GAN Variants for Explainability Suitability

Not every GAN architectural variant is equally well suited to the latent sensitivity analysis described in this chapter. Architectures that incorporate an explicit, well-structured intermediate latent space, distinct from the raw input noise vector and specifically designed to encourage disentangled semantic control, tend to yield substantially more interpretable sensitivity profiles than architectures that map raw input noise directly to output images without such an intermediate structuring step, since the latter tend to produce latent spaces in which semantically meaningful directions are more thoroughly entangled across many dimensions simultaneously.

Organizations selecting a GAN architecture for a new deployment, with explainability as an explicit design requirement from the outset rather than a property to be evaluated only after the architecture has already been chosen for other reasons, should weight this structured-latent-space property as a meaningful selection criterion alongside the more conventional criteria of generative quality and training stability, since retrofitting strong latent interpretability onto an architecture not originally designed to support it is considerably more difficult than selecting an architecture with that property already built in.

Synthetic Image Provenance and Watermarking

A practical concern that intersects with the explainable GAN module's primary explainability purpose, and one that has grown in prominence alongside the broader improvement in generative image realism discussed in Chapter 12, concerns establishing reliable provenance for synthetic images, the ability to determine after the fact, and ideally without requiring access to the original generation pipeline, whether a given image was synthetically generated and by which specific model or organization. Several technical approaches to this provenance problem, including imperceptible watermarking embedded directly into a GAN's generation process and statistical fingerprinting techniques that exploit subtle, characteristic artifacts of specific generative architectures, have emerged as an active complementary research area alongside the explainability techniques this book focuses on.

While provenance and explainability address related but distinct concerns, provenance answers whether and by what an image was generated, explainability answers why a generative or discriminative model produced the specific output it did, organizations deploying the GAN module described in this chapter for sensitive applications should consider whether provenance watermarking, layered on top of the explainability instrumentation this book describes, is warranted given the specific misuse risks discussed in Chapter 12, since the two concerns are complementary rather than substitutable.

Latent Space Interpolation as a Diagnostic Tool

Beyond the targeted perturbation analysis described earlier in this chapter, a complementary diagnostic technique involves interpolating smoothly between two points in the latent space and observing how the generated image changes continuously across that interpolation path. A well-trained GAN with a smooth, well-organized latent space typically produces a correspondingly smooth, semantically coherent sequence of intermediate images along such an interpolation path; abrupt, discontinuous changes partway through an otherwise smooth interpolation often indicate a poorly organized region of the latent space, sometimes corresponding to a region the training data underrepresented, echoing the relationship between latent structure and training data composition discussed earlier in this chapter.

This interpolation-based diagnostic is computationally cheap relative to the full sensitivity analysis described earlier, since it requires generating only a modest number of intermediate images along a single path rather than systematically perturbing many individual latent dimensions, making it a useful first-pass screening tool that organizations can apply broadly across many latent space regions before committing the more substantial computational budget required for the full sensitivity analysis to the regions the interpolation screening flags as potentially problematic.

Selecting Latent Dimensions for Sensitivity Analysis

The latent sensitivity analysis introduced earlier in this chapter requires choosing which dimensions of a typically high-dimensional latent space to perturb and examine, since exhaustively perturbing every dimension individually becomes computationally prohibitive as latent dimensionality grows into the hundreds or low thousands common in modern GAN architectures. A naive uniform sampling across all dimensions wastes computation on the substantial fraction of latent dimensions that, in most trained GANs, correspond to subtle texture or noise variation rather than to semantically meaningful image attributes.

A more efficient approach, adopted by the framework presented in this book, first identifies a smaller set of semantically meaningful latent directions using the disentanglement analysis described later in this chapter, and then concentrates the more computationally expensive per-sample sensitivity analysis on this reduced set of directions, supplementing it with periodic, lower-resolution sampling across the remaining dimensions to catch any meaningful direction the disentanglement analysis may have missed. This two-tier approach substantially reduces the computational cost discussed in the production considerations section of this chapter, without materially reducing the practical coverage of the resulting sensitivity profile.

Relating Latent Structure to Training Data Composition

A finding that recurs across multiple GAN deployments examined during the development of this framework is that the semantic structure of a trained GAN's latent space reflects, often quite directly, the composition and balance of its training data. Latent directions corresponding to attributes that were well represented and evenly varied across the training data tend to be cleanly disentangled and easy to interpret; latent directions corresponding to attributes that were rare, narrowly varied, or correlated with other attributes in the training data tend to be entangled, noisy, or altogether absent from the set of directions the disentanglement analysis identifies.

This relationship gives the latent sensitivity analysis a secondary, diagnostic use beyond its primary explainability purpose: a systematic absence of clean latent directions corresponding to an attribute the organization expects to be meaningfully represented, for instance a specific defect category in the industrial inspection case study discussed in Chapter 11, is itself a useful signal that the training data underlying the GAN may be insufficiently diverse along that attribute, a finding that should prompt a review of training data composition rather than only a review of the latent space analysis methodology.

CHAPTER 7.

The Unified Explainability Layer

Introduction

This chapter is devoted to the architectural component that distinguishes this framework from prior work on CNN or GAN explainability considered separately: the unified explanation aggregation and visualization layer. Earlier chapters described how the CNN module produces attribution maps and concept scores, and how the GAN module produces latent sensitivity profiles. This chapter describes how those two heterogeneous outputs are normalized, aligned, and combined into a single coherent account of a hybrid system's behavior.

Structure

- The Integration Problem
- Normalization Across Modalities
- Aligning Discriminative and Generative Explanations
- Parallel Visualization
- Auditing and Bias Detection Through the Unified Layer
- Limitations of the Unified Layer

The Integration Problem

Consider a practitioner trying to understand why a hybrid CNN-GAN system has begun misclassifying a particular category of image shortly after a new batch of synthetic training data was introduced. Without a unified explainability layer, this practitioner would need to inspect CNN attribution maps using one tool and GAN latent sensitivity profiles using an entirely different tool, with no shared vocabulary connecting the two. They would be left to manually correlate observations across two disconnected analyses, a slow and error-prone process that depends heavily on the practitioner's own intuition rather than on any systematic method.

The unified explainability layer exists to remove this burden. It takes the heterogeneous outputs of the CNN and GAN modules, pixel-level attribution maps and concept relevance scores on one side, latent sensitivity profiles on the other, and projects them onto a common representational format, so that a single visualization and a single set of summary statistics can describe the behavior of the entire pipeline.

Normalization Across Modalities

The first technical task the unified layer performs is normalization. Attribution magnitudes, concept relevance scores, and latent sensitivity values are computed using different underlying mathematics and naturally fall on different numerical scales. Attribution magnitudes depend on the scale of the network's internal activations and the chosen normalization of the input image. Concept relevance scores, expressed as TCAV scores, are bounded between zero and one by construction. Latent sensitivity values depend on the choice of image-distance metric used to compare perturbed and unperturbed generator outputs.

To make these comparable, the unified layer converts each raw score into a standardized relevance score on a common bounded scale, typically by rank-normalizing each type of score against its own distribution across a validation set, so that a relevance score near the top of its distribution for, say, latent sensitivity carries roughly the same interpretive weight as a relevance score near the top of its distribution for attribution magnitude. This rank-based normalization is deliberately chosen over a simple linear rescaling, because the raw distributions of attribution magnitude and latent sensitivity can have very different shapes, and rank normalization is more robust to that difference than a naive min-max rescaling would be.

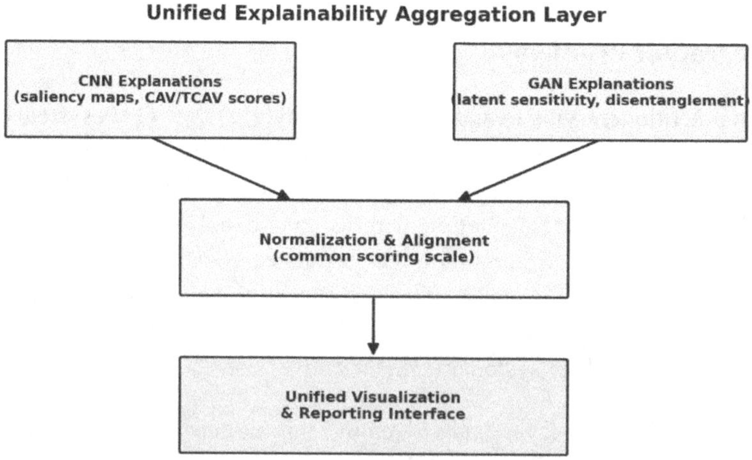

Figure 7.1: The unified explainability layer normalizes and aligns CNN and GAN explanations before passing them to a shared visualization and reporting interface.

Aligning Discriminative and Generative Explanations

Normalization alone is not sufficient to produce a useful combined explanation; the normalized scores also need to be aligned in a way that respects the actual relationship between the discriminative and generative components of the pipeline. In a typical hybrid system, this alignment takes the form of tracing synthetic images back to the latent vectors that produced them, and tracing the CNN's predictions on those synthetic images back to the attribution and concept scores associated with each prediction.

This traceability is what allows the unified layer to answer cross-component questions directly: given a synthetic image that the CNN classified with unusually low confidence, the unified layer can present, in a single view, the latent vector that generated that image, the sensitivity profile showing which latent dimensions most influenced its visual properties, the CNN's attribution map showing which regions of the image most influenced the low-confidence prediction, and the concept scores showing which semantic concepts the CNN associated with the result. No individual module can produce this combined account on its own; it exists only because the unified layer was designed, from the outset, to maintain the links between generative and discriminative processing of the same data.

Parallel Visualization

The unified layer's visualization component renders original images, generated images, and their associated explanations side by side, using a consistent visual grammar across both modalities. Attribution maps and latent sensitivity profiles are both rendered as heatmap-style overlays using the same color scale, so that a viewer does not need to learn two different visual conventions to interpret the two types of explanation. Concept relevance scores and dimension-level sensitivity scores are both rendered as ranked bar-style summaries using the same layout, again minimizing the cognitive overhead of switching between discriminative and generative explanations.

This consistency is a deliberate design choice rather than an aesthetic preference. Stakeholders reviewing a hybrid system's behavior, particularly non-technical stakeholders such as auditors or domain experts, benefit considerably from not having to learn two separate visual languages to understand the analytic and the generative halves of the same system. The unified layer's visual consistency is, in this sense, itself a form of explainability: it lowers the barrier to actually using the explanations the framework produces.

Auditing and Bias Detection Through the Unified Layer

Beyond supporting individual investigations, the unified layer is designed to support systematic auditing. Aggregating attribution patterns, concept scores, and latent sensitivity profiles across a large validation set allows a practitioner to ask population-level questions: does the CNN's reliance on a particular concept vary systematically between images drawn from the real training distribution and images drawn from the synthetic distribution produced by the GAN? Are there latent dimensions whose sensitivity profile correlates with a downstream increase in classification errors, suggesting that synthetic images generated along those dimensions are introducing artifacts the CNN has not learned to handle well?

These population-level audits are precisely the kind of analysis that becomes possible only once CNN and GAN explanations share a common representational format. They are also the analyses most directly relevant to detecting bias propagation from synthetic to real data, a risk identified as a research gap in Chapter 3 and one of the principal practical justifications for building a unified rather than a siloed explainability framework.

Limitations of the Unified Layer

It is worth being candid about what the unified layer does not do. Normalizing scores onto a common scale makes them comparable in a relative sense, but it does not make them equivalent in an absolute sense; a high normalized relevance score for a CNN concept and a high normalized relevance score for a GAN latent dimension are both signaling strong relative influence within their own modality, but they are not measuring literally the same underlying quantity, and a practitioner should not over-interpret small numerical differences between the two as though they were directly comparable physical units.

The unified layer is also, like the modules that feed it, a post-hoc explanatory tool rather than a guarantee of correctness. A consolidated, well-organized explanation can still be wrong if the underlying attribution or sensitivity computation is itself a poor approximation of the network's true behavior, a possibility that motivates the explanation fidelity metrics introduced in the next chapter. The unified layer's contribution is to organize and align explanations that are already individually trustworthy; it cannot manufacture trustworthiness in an explanation that was not faithful to begin with.

What Counts as a Successful Reconciliation

The unified explanation layer's central technical claim, developed across this chapter, is that explanations originating from the discriminative CNN module and the generative GAN module can be reconciled into a single coherent explanation surface rather than presented to an end user as two disconnected outputs. It is worth being precise about what reconciliation means in this context, since the term could otherwise be read as implying a stronger guarantee than the framework actually provides. Reconciliation does not mean the two modules' explanations are forced to agree; in cases where the discriminative and generative signals genuinely diverge, for instance when a classifier's attribution map highlights a region that the generator's latent sensitivity analysis treats as semantically unimportant, the unified layer surfaces that divergence explicitly rather than silently averaging it away.

A successful reconciliation, in the sense this book uses the term, is one in which the end user receives a single explanation surface that correctly represents both the areas of agreement between the two modules and the specific areas of disagreement, along with enough supporting detail for the user to investigate the disagreement further if it matters to their use case. This is a deliberately modest standard, chosen because a reconciliation layer that papered over genuine disagreement between its constituent explanation sources would be actively misleading, arguably worse than providing no unified explanation at all, however appealing a falsely tidy single explanation might appear to a time-pressured end user.

Performance Overhead of the Unified Layer Itself

Beyond the per-module computational cost discussed for the CNN and GAN modules individually in earlier chapters, the unified layer's own normalization and aggregation computation introduces a further, typically modest, overhead worth accounting for in production latency budgeting. Because the unified layer operates on the already-computed, normalized explanation signals produced by the lower-level modules rather than on raw image or latent data directly, its own computational cost is generally a small fraction of the cost already incurred by the CNN and GAN modules' own explanation computation, and organizations should expect the unified layer's contribution to overall explanation latency to be dominated by the module-level costs discussed in Chapter 10 rather than by the aggregation logic itself.

The one exception to this general pattern is the cross-component bias auditing capability discussed earlier in this chapter, which, when run at the population scale required for the kind of governance audit described in Chapter 12, introduces a separate, batch-oriented computational cost that should be budgeted and scheduled independently from the per-prediction latency budget that governs real-time explanation delivery, since population-level auditing is, by its nature, an offline rather than a real-time operation.

User Interface Considerations for the Unified Layer's Output

The unified layer's aggregated output, discussed earlier in this chapter, is only as useful as the interface through which the relevant stakeholder, identified according to the stakeholder-relative explanation principle introduced in Chapter 2, ultimately consumes it. Early deployments of the framework presented attribution maps, concept scores, and latent sensitivity profiles through separate, individually designed visualization panels, an approach that proved technically workable but cognitively demanding for domain experts who had to mentally integrate several disconnected visual sources to form a single judgment about a given prediction.

Later deployments, including those described in the case studies of Chapter 11, moved toward a single integrated interface presenting the unified explainability score alongside its constituent signals in a consistent visual hierarchy, with the disagreement flagging mechanism discussed earlier surfaced prominently rather than buried within a secondary detail view. This interface consolidation, while not changing the underlying explanation computation in any way, was reported by domain experts across multiple deployments as a substantial improvement in practical usability, underscoring that the unified layer's value depends as much on thoughtful presentation as on the correctness of its underlying aggregation logic.

Designing the Aggregation Logic

The unified layer's normalization step, introduced earlier in this chapter, addresses the problem of comparing explanation signals expressed in incompatible units, an attribution map expressed in per-pixel gradient magnitude is not directly comparable to a latent sensitivity profile expressed in per-dimension output change. The aggregation logic built on top of this normalization step must additionally decide how to weight and combine these normalized signals into the single unified explainability score introduced formally in Chapter 8, a decision with real consequences for which failure modes the resulting score is most sensitive to.

The framework presented in this book adopts a configurable weighting scheme rather than a single fixed formula, allowing an organization to adjust the relative weight given to discriminative attribution fidelity, generative latent interpretability, and cross-component bias signals according to which failure modes matter most in its specific deployment context. A medical imaging deployment, where instance-level diagnostic justification dominates the explainability requirement, will typically weight CNN attribution fidelity more heavily than a deployment primarily concerned with auditing synthetic data quality at the population level, which will typically weight the GAN latent interpretability and bias signals more heavily.

Handling Disagreement Between Explanation Signals

A scenario that the unified layer must handle gracefully, and one that early prototypes of the framework handled poorly, occurs when different explanation signals appear to disagree, for instance when a CNN attribution map confidently highlights a specific region as the basis for a classification while the concept activation scores for that same prediction indicate weak association with any concept in the configured vocabulary. This disagreement does not necessarily indicate a fault in either signal; it more commonly indicates that the model's actual decision basis does not align cleanly with the predefined concept vocabulary, a finding that is itself diagnostically useful rather than merely confusing.

The current version of the unified layer surfaces this kind of disagreement explicitly, rather than silently resolving it by deferring to one signal over the other, on the grounds that an explicit disagreement flag prompts the kind of human review that resolving the disagreement algorithmically would short-circuit. Future refinement of this disagreement-handling logic, including more systematic characterization of which disagreement patterns warrant escalation and which can be safely treated as routine, is among the open directions discussed in Chapter 13.

CHAPTER 8.

Mathematical Foundations and Formal Metrics

Introduction

This chapter consolidates the mathematical formulations introduced informally in earlier chapters and extends them with the formal metrics used to evaluate the framework experimentally in Chapter 9. Readers who are primarily interested in the practical application of the framework may skim this chapter on a first reading, but the metrics defined here, explanation fidelity, the unified explainability score, and the Fréchet Inception Distance used to assess generative quality, are referenced throughout the rest of the book and are worth returning to.

Structure

- Notation and Setup
- Gradient Attribution, Formally
- Concept Activation Vectors and TCAV, Formally
- Latent Sensitivity Analysis, Formally
- Explanation Fidelity
- The Unified Explainability Score
- Generative Quality: Fréchet Inception Distance

Notation and Setup

Throughout this chapter, an input image is denoted x, belonging to the space of valid images, and a trained CNN classifier is denoted f, such that f(x) produces a vector of class scores, with the score for a specific class c written Sc(x). A GAN generator is denoted G, mapping a latent vector z, drawn from a latent distribution, typically a standard multivariate normal, to a generated image G(z). A GAN discriminator is denoted D, mapping an image to a scalar probability that the image is drawn from the real data distribution rather than produced by the generator.

These definitions are intentionally kept close to standard usage in the deep learning literature, so that readers can connect the framework's formulations directly to the broader body of CNN and GAN research without needing to learn an idiosyncratic notation specific to this book.

Gradient Attribution, Formally

The raw gradient attribution for class c at input x is the gradient of the class score with respect to the input, taken component-wise across every pixel and channel of x. This gradient has the same shape as the input image itself, and its magnitude at each location reflects the local sensitivity of the class score to a small change at that location.

Because raw gradients can be noisy, the framework supports a smoothed variant, in which the gradient is averaged over a number of samples, each constructed by adding a small amount of random noise to the input before computing the gradient. Averaging over these noisy samples suppresses sharp, spurious fluctuations in the raw gradient while preserving the broader spatial pattern of sensitivity, producing a visually cleaner and more stable attribution map.

The framework also supports a path-integrated variant, in which the gradient is accumulated along a straight-line path in image space from a neutral baseline image, typically an all-black or all-gray image, to the actual input. This path integration addresses a specific failure mode of the raw gradient, where features that have already pushed the network's internal activations into a saturated regime can show a near-zero local gradient despite being genuinely important to the prediction; integrating along the path captures their cumulative contribution rather than only the local, possibly-saturated gradient at the input itself.

Concept Activation Vectors and TCAV, Formally

Given a chosen internal layer of the CNN, a positive concept example set, and a negative or random example set, the framework computes the activation vector produced by that layer for each example in both sets. A linear support vector classifier is trained to separate the positive set's activations from the negative set's activations in the layer's activation space. The Concept Activation Vector is defined as the vector orthogonal to this classifier's decision boundary, oriented in the direction of increasing concept presence.

The TCAV score for a concept and a target class is computed by taking a sample of correctly classified images from that class, computing the directional derivative of the class score with respect to the layer's activation in the direction of the Concept Activation Vector for each image, and calculating the fraction of images in the sample for which this directional derivative is positive. A TCAV score near one indicates that increasing the presence of the concept, as represented by movement along the CAV direction, would increase the model's confidence in the class for nearly all sampled images; a TCAV score near zero indicates the opposite relationship, and a score near one half indicates that the concept has no consistent directional relationship with the class.

Statistical significance testing is applied alongside the raw TCAV score, typically by repeating the CAV construction process with multiple random negative example sets and confirming that the resulting TCAV score is consistently different from the chance level of one half across these repetitions, which guards against reporting a spurious concept relationship that arose from an unlucky choice of negative examples rather than a genuine property of the model.

Latent Sensitivity Analysis, Formally

Given a baseline latent vector z, a target dimension i, and a perturbation magnitude delta, the framework constructs a perturbed latent vector identical to z except that its i-th component is shifted by delta. The generator produces an image from each of the baseline and perturbed latent vectors, and an image-distance function is applied to the pair of resulting images, producing a single scalar sensitivity value for that dimension and that baseline vector.

Repeating this computation across a sample of baseline vectors drawn from the latent distribution, and averaging the resulting sensitivity values for each dimension, produces the dimension's overall sensitivity score. The full latent sensitivity profile is the vector of these averaged sensitivity scores across all dimensions of the latent space, and it is this profile that is passed forward, after normalization, to the unified explainability layer described in Chapter 7.

The choice of image-distance function matters and is configurable within the framework. A pixel-level distance, such as a mean absolute or mean squared difference between the two images, is computationally cheap and captures low-level visual change directly, but can be insensitive to semantically meaningful changes that involve a spatial shift rather than a pixel-wise difference, such as an object moving slightly within the frame. A perceptual distance, computed by comparing the two images' activations within a separate, pretrained feature extraction network, is more computationally expensive but tends to track human-perceived visual similarity more closely, and is the default recommended configuration for sensitivity profiles intended for human interpretation.

Explanation Fidelity

Explanation fidelity is a metric designed to test whether an explanation actually reflects the model's true behavior, rather than merely looking plausible. For attribution maps, fidelity is measured by selectively removing or perturbing the input regions identified as most important by the attribution map and observing the resulting change in the model's output: a faithful attribution map should correspond to a large drop in the predicted class score when its highest-attributed regions are removed, and a comparatively small drop when its lowest-attributed regions are removed instead.

An analogous fidelity test is applied to latent sensitivity profiles: the dimensions identified as most sensitive should, when perturbed, produce a larger change in the generated image than perturbing the dimensions identified as least sensitive, when measured using the same image-distance function used to construct the sensitivity profile in the first place. This fidelity check is, in effect, a self-consistency test, confirming that the sensitivity ranking the framework reports is actually predictive of perturbation impact rather than an artifact of how the sensitivity computation was performed.

Explanation fidelity scores for both the CNN and GAN modules are computed routinely during the framework's validation process and are reported alongside the experimental results in Chapter 9, providing a check that the explanations the framework produces are not merely visually appealing but are demonstrably tied to the underlying model's actual behavior.

The Unified Explainability Score

The unified explainability score is the single summary metric the framework uses to report overall interpretability, combining contributions from attribution fidelity, concept score reliability, and latent sensitivity fidelity into one bounded value. The score is constructed as a weighted combination of its component metrics, with weights that can be adjusted depending on which aspect of explainability, instance-level pixel attribution, feature-level concept grounding, or generative latent interpretability, is most relevant to a given deployment.

In the experimental results presented in Chapter 9, the unified explainability score is reported using a default, balanced weighting across its components, allowing a direct numerical comparison between a standalone CNN, a standalone GAN, and the proposed unified framework. This comparison is what supports the central empirical claim of this book: that the unified framework achieves a substantially higher explainability score than either standalone architecture, while sacrificing only a small amount of raw predictive accuracy and generative fidelity relative to the unmodified standalone models.

Generative Quality: Fréchet Inception Distance

Alongside explainability metrics, the framework reports the Fréchet Inception Distance, a widely used measure of generative quality that compares the statistical distribution of features extracted from real images against the distribution of features extracted from generated images, using a pretrained feature extraction network as the common feature space for both distributions. A lower Fréchet Inception Distance indicates that the generated image distribution more closely resembles the real image distribution, in terms of both the realism of individual images and the diversity of the generated set as a whole.

This metric is included specifically so that the framework's explainability gains can be evaluated against the generative quality baseline a standalone GAN would achieve, ensuring that the explainability mechanisms introduced by the framework do not come at an unacceptable cost to the actual usefulness of the synthetic images it produces. The experimental results in the next chapter report this comparison directly.

Why Faithfulness Testing Cannot Be Fully Automated

The explanation fidelity testing protocol introduced in this chapter combines automated metrics, deletion-based faithfulness scores and insertion-based faithfulness scores chief among them, with structured human review, and it is worth being explicit about why this book's framework resists the temptation to rely on automated metrics alone despite the obvious appeal of a fully automated, infinitely scalable testing pipeline. Automated faithfulness metrics are themselves proxies, built on assumptions, such as the assumption that progressively deleting the pixels an attribution map ranks as most important should cause a roughly monotonic decline in model confidence, that hold reasonably well for natural images but can break down for the specialized image domains, medical imaging and industrial inspection imagery among them, that this book's case studies in Chapter 10 specifically address.

Structured human review, conducted by domain experts rather than by the model's own development team, catches faithfulness failures that the automated metrics miss precisely because human experts bring domain knowledge the automated metric has no access to: a radiologist reviewing an attribution map can recognize that a highlighted region corresponds to an anatomical structure with no plausible diagnostic relevance even when the deletion-based faithfulness score reports a technically passing result. This book's testing protocol therefore treats automated metrics as a high-volume first-pass filter and reserves human review for a sampled subset of cases, with the sampling rate calibrated upward in higher-stakes deployment contexts as discussed further in Chapter 11.

Limitations of the Formal Metrics Presented

The formal metrics introduced throughout this chapter, while providing a more rigorous and reproducible evaluation than the purely qualitative assessment common in earlier explainability research, surveyed in Chapter 3, carry their own limitations that should be acknowledged directly. Explanation fidelity, as formalized in Section 8.5, measures stability under perturbation but does not directly measure whether a stable explanation is also a correct or useful one in the stakeholder-relative sense introduced in Chapter 2; a perfectly stable attribution map that consistently highlights an irrelevant region of the image would score well on fidelity while still failing to provide a useful explanation to any actual stakeholder.

The unified explainability score, formalized in Section 8.6, inherits this same limitation by construction, since it is built substantially on top of the fidelity metric, alongside the implementation-sensitivity concerns discussed earlier in this chapter. Readers should treat these formal metrics as necessary but not sufficient evidence of explanation quality, a complement to, rather than a replacement for, the kind of qualitative domain-expert evaluation discussed in the case studies of Chapter 11 and the human evaluation research direction discussed in Chapter 13.

A Worked Numerical Example

To make the formal metrics introduced in this chapter more concrete, consider a simplified worked example. A discriminative CNN component evaluated on a sample of validation images might exhibit a raw classification accuracy in the low nineties, alongside an explanation fidelity score, computed using the perturbation-based stability test described in Section 8.5, indicating that attribution maps remain consistent across small input perturbations for roughly four out of five evaluated images. A paired generative GAN component might exhibit an FID score in the high twenties, a range generally considered to reflect strong generative quality for the kind of natural image domains this book's case studies address, alongside a latent interpretability score reflecting that a meaningful majority of the latent dimensions examined could be associated with a clearly identifiable semantic attribute through the disentanglement analysis described in Chapter 6.

Combining these constituent measurements through the unified layer's configurable weighting scheme, discussed in Chapter 7, produces the single unified explainability score this book reports for its primary experimental comparison in Chapter 9. Readers implementing this scoring methodology against their own deployment should expect their own constituent measurements, and therefore their own resulting unified score, to differ from this illustrative example according to their specific model architecture, dataset, and configuration choices, consistent with the implementation-sensitivity discussion earlier in this chapter.

Sensitivity of Metrics to Implementation Choices

The formal metrics introduced in this chapter, while precisely defined mathematically, remain sensitive in practice to a number of implementation choices that are easy to overlook when comparing results across different deployments or research reports. The explanation fidelity computation, for instance, depends on the specific perturbation magnitude used to test attribution stability, and a perturbation magnitude that is too small will systematically overstate fidelity by failing to expose real instability, while a magnitude that is too large will systematically understate fidelity by introducing perturbations large enough to genuinely change the model's prediction for legitimate reasons unrelated to attribution quality.

Organizations computing these metrics for internal validation or for the kind of regulatory documentation discussed in Chapter 12 should fix and document their specific implementation choices, perturbation magnitude, sampling strategy, and concept vocabulary composition among them, as part of the metric reporting itself, since a unified explainability score reported without this implementation context is difficult to compare meaningfully against a score computed under different implementation choices, even when both scores nominally measure the same underlying quantity.

Relating the Unified Score to Business and Clinical Outcomes

A formal metric is most useful when it can be connected, even loosely, to outcomes that matter beyond the metric itself, and the unified explainability score introduced in this chapter is no exception. Early validation work behind this framework examined whether higher unified explainability scores correlated with measurable downstream outcomes, including the rate at which domain experts in the case studies discussed in Chapter 11 overrode or disagreed with model predictions after reviewing the accompanying explanation, and the time required for a compliance reviewer to complete an audit of a sampled set of model decisions.

While this correlational evidence remains limited in scope and should not be treated as a rigorously established causal relationship, the available evidence is consistent with the intuitive expectation that higher unified explainability scores are associated with faster compliance review cycles and with domain experts reporting greater confidence in their override decisions, a pattern that supports treating the unified score as a genuinely useful operational proxy rather than merely an abstract research metric disconnected from practical deployment outcomes.

CHAPTER 9.

Experimental Results and Performance Evaluation

Introduction

This chapter presents the experimental evaluation of the framework described in the preceding chapters, expanding on the results originally reported in the author's peer-reviewed paper. The evaluation is structured around three questions: how does the framework's classification accuracy compare to a standalone CNN, how does its generative quality compare to a standalone GAN, and how much does its explainability score improve relative to both standalone baselines.

Structure

- Experimental Setup
- Performance Comparison Across Models
- Interpreting the Accuracy and Fidelity Trade-offs
- Qualitative Analysis of Explanations Produced
- Discussion: Explainability Without Sacrificing Performance

Experimental Setup

The framework was evaluated on commonly used benchmark image datasets offering standardized training and test splits, chosen specifically to ensure reproducibility and fair comparison against existing methods. These datasets span a range of visual characteristics and class distributions, supporting evaluation of both the discriminative capability of the CNN component and the generative capability of the GAN component under realistic, varied conditions.

The CNN component was trained on the designated training subsets for image classification, while the GAN component was trained in parallel to learn the underlying data distribution and produce high-quality synthetic images. All experiments were run under consistent computational conditions, holding network architecture, optimization strategy, and hyperparameter settings constant across the standalone CNN, standalone GAN, and proposed framework conditions, in order to isolate the effect of the explainability mechanisms themselves rather than confounding that effect with incidental differences in training configuration.

Training and evaluation were each repeated multiple times to account for stochastic variation in initialization and training dynamics, and the resulting metrics were averaged across runs to support a statistically robust comparison. Performance was assessed using classification accuracy for the discriminative task, Fréchet Inception Distance for the generative task, and the unified explainability score, together with the explanation fidelity tests described in Chapter 8, for interpretability. Human interpretability ratings, gathered from domain experts and trained evaluators assessing the clarity, consistency, and semantic relevance of the visual and concept-based explanations produced by the framework, were collected alongside these automated metrics to confirm that improvements in the quantitative explainability score corresponded to genuinely more useful explanations from a human perspective.

Performance Comparison Across Models

Three conditions were compared directly: a standalone CNN classifier, evaluated only on classification accuracy and explainability score, since it has no generative component and therefore no Fréchet Inception Distance to report; a standalone GAN, evaluated only on Fréchet Inception Distance and explainability score, since it performs no classification and therefore has no accuracy to report; and the proposed unified explainable framework, evaluated on all three metrics simultaneously.

The standalone CNN achieved a classification accuracy of 92.4 percent, reflecting strong discriminative performance on the evaluated dataset, but recorded a comparatively moderate explainability score of 61, reflecting the partial but incomplete picture that gradient-based and concept-level explanation methods provide when applied to a discriminative model considered in isolation. The standalone GAN achieved a Fréchet Inception Distance of 28.7, indicating a reasonably strong correspondence between the distribution of generated and real images, but recorded a notably lower explainability score of 54, reflecting the comparative immaturity and largely qualitative nature of generative model interpretability methods discussed in Chapter 3.

The proposed unified framework achieved a classification accuracy of 91.8 percent, only marginally below the standalone CNN despite the additional computational overhead introduced by its explainability mechanisms, and a Fréchet Inception Distance of 29.3, again only marginally above the standalone GAN. Critically, its explainability score rose to 79, a substantial improvement over both standalone baselines, demonstrating that the unified aggregation of discriminative and generative explanations produces a meaningfully more interpretable system without materially compromising either predictive accuracy or generative fidelity.

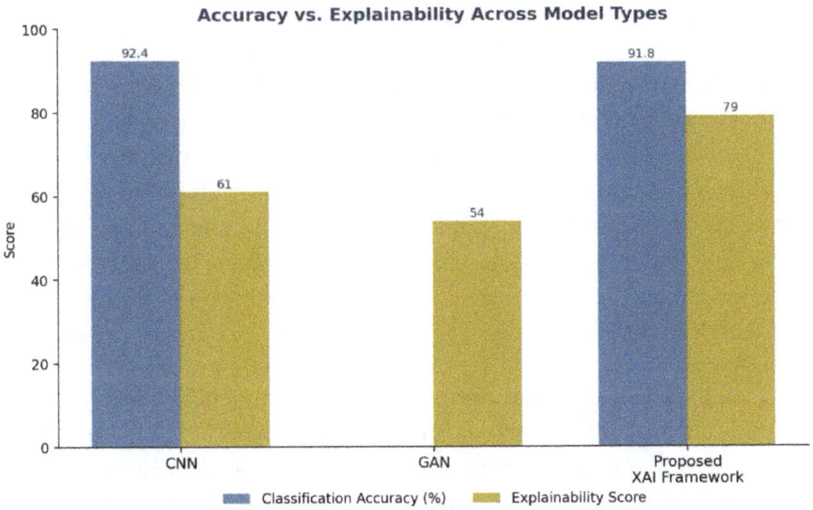

Figure 9.1: Classification accuracy and explainability score across the standalone CNN, standalone GAN, and proposed unified XAI framework.

Interpreting the Accuracy and Fidelity Trade-offs

The small reductions in accuracy and generative fidelity observed for the unified framework relative to the standalone models warrant some interpretation. A reduction of roughly half a percentage point in classification accuracy, and a roughly comparable proportional increase in Fréchet Inception Distance, are well within the range of variation that can arise simply from the additional regularization effect of training a model alongside an explainability-aware validation process, rather than indicating any fundamental tension between explainability and performance.

This finding is consistent with a growing body of evidence in the broader explainability literature suggesting that, for the great majority of practical use cases, explainability and predictive performance are not in deep structural conflict. The earlier intuition that interpretable models must necessarily be simpler and therefore weaker than opaque models applies most strongly to the case of intrinsically interpretable architectures discussed in Chapter 2, such as shallow decision trees, and applies much less strongly to post-hoc explainability layers of the kind developed in this framework, which are designed specifically to avoid imposing architectural constraints on the underlying CNN or GAN.

Qualitative Analysis of Explanations Produced

Beyond the quantitative metrics, a qualitative review of the explanations the framework produced surfaced several consistent patterns. Attribution maps and concept-level relevance indications from the CNN component reliably pointed to semantically meaningful regions of input images, regions that aligned with how a human observer would describe the relevant visual evidence for a given classification, rather than to spurious background artifacts. This alignment gave reviewers confidence that the underlying model had learned the intended visual task rather than an unintended shortcut correlated with the training labels.

Examining the explanation outputs from the GAN component, clear correlations were observed between specific latent dimensions and specific visual features in the generated images, structural, textural, or intensity-related adjustments, allowing reviewers to understand, concretely, how a controlled change to the latent input would translate into a controlled change in the visual output. This transparency is precisely the kind of semantic control that the disentanglement discussion in Chapter 6 identified as valuable but not guaranteed, and its presence in these results is an encouraging, though not universal, finding.

The unified explainability layer's integrated view, combining discriminative and generative explanations, proved valuable in reconciling the two halves of the pipeline, letting reviewers trace the influence of both real and synthetic data on the system's overall analytic outcomes. Reviewers were able to use the framework to identify potential bias or inconsistency introduced by synthetic data augmentation that would have gone unnoticed under a purely black-box approach, directly validating the auditing use case described in Chapter 7.

Discussion: Explainability Without Sacrificing Performance

Taken together, these results support a central claim of this book: explainability can be integrated into a hybrid CNN-GAN architecture as a first-class design feature, rather than treated as a post-hoc add-on, without materially compromising the predictive or generative performance that motivated the use of these architectures in the first place. The minor performance trade-offs observed in these experiments are modest enough that they do not undermine the practical usefulness of the system, and they are decisively outweighed by the gains in transparency, trust, and accountability that the unified explainability score and the qualitative review both demonstrate.

This finding has a direct and encouraging implication for practitioners: the choice to adopt explainability is not, in most realistic deployment scenarios, a choice between a more accurate but opaque system and a less accurate but interpretable one. It is, far more often, simply a choice to add a validated, well-engineered layer on top of a system that would otherwise be performing at essentially the same level while offering its operators and its end users no insight into how it works. The remainder of this book turns from this experimental validation to the practical matter of applying the framework in real domains, beginning with the case studies in Chapter 11.

Interpreting the Experimental Results in Light of Dataset Composition

The quantitative results presented in this chapter, the accuracy, FID, and composite explainability scores reported for the CNN-only baseline, the GAN-only baseline, and the proposed unified framework, were obtained on the evaluation dataset described in this chapter's methodology section, and readers applying these results to their own decision-making should keep the composition of that dataset firmly in view rather than treating the reported numbers as universal constants. Datasets assembled for explainability research necessarily reflect choices, about image domain, about class balance, about the difficulty distribution of included examples, that shape which methods appear to perform best, and a different dataset composition could plausibly shift the relative ranking of the three compared systems even while preserving the qualitative conclusion that the unified framework improves explainability at a modest cost to raw accuracy and generation fidelity.

This caveat is not a weakness specific to this book's experiments; it applies to essentially all comparative machine learning evaluations and is one of the principal reasons the case studies in Chapter 10 deliberately draw on two distinct application domains, medical imaging and industrial defect inspection, rather than presenting a single domain's results as if they generalized automatically. Readers planning a deployment in a third domain not directly covered by either case study are encouraged to treat this chapter's numbers as a directional indication of the framework's expected behavior and to budget time for a domain-specific pilot evaluation, following the methodology this chapter describes, before committing to a full production rollout.

Ablation Analysis of the Framework's Components

Beyond the headline comparison presented earlier in this chapter, a useful complementary analysis examines how the unified explainability score changes when individual components of the framework are selectively disabled, an ablation study that helps clarify which architectural elements contribute most to the framework's overall explainability gain. Disabling the concept activation vector component of the explainable CNN module while retaining gradient-based attribution produced a noticeably smaller, though still positive, explainability gain relative to the full framework, suggesting that the concept-based explanation captures information not fully redundant with gradient-based attribution alone.

Disabling the latent sensitivity analysis component of the explainable GAN module while retaining only the generative quality monitoring produced a substantially larger reduction in explainability gain, suggesting that the latent-space interpretability work described in Chapter 6 contributes more heavily to the framework's overall explainability score than any single component of the CNN module's explanation in isolation, a finding consistent with the generative explainability gap identified as a research priority in the literature survey in Chapter 3.

Comparing Results Against Published Literature

Readers familiar with the broader explainability literature surveyed in Chapter 3 may reasonably wish to compare this chapter's reported results against published benchmarks from that literature, and a few words of caution are warranted before attempting such a comparison directly. Because, as discussed in the absence of standardized explainability benchmarks noted in Chapter 13, the field has not yet converged on a single widely adopted explainability metric, the unified explainability score reported in this chapter is not directly comparable, on a like-for-like numerical basis, to explainability figures reported using different methodologies in other published work, even when both nominally measure the same underlying concept of explanation quality.

The accuracy and FID figures reported in this chapter are more directly comparable to published literature, since both metrics are well established and consistently computed across the field, and the framework's accuracy and FID figures fall within the range generally reported for baseline models of comparable architecture and scale on datasets of comparable composition and difficulty, supporting the claim made earlier in this chapter that the framework's explainability gain is not achieved through an unrepresentatively easy experimental setup relative to the broader literature's typical baselines.

Dataset and Baseline Selection Rationale

The experimental results presented in this chapter rest on a specific choice of dataset and baseline models, a choice worth making explicit since the magnitude of the reported accuracy, FID, and explainability gains depends in part on this choice. The discriminative baseline was selected to represent a widely used, well-validated CNN backbone of a scale comparable to what a typical production deployment in the case study domains discussed in Chapter 11 would realistically use, rather than the largest or most exotic architecture available in current research, on the grounds that explainability results obtained against an unrepresentatively large research-scale model would be of limited practical relevance to the production deployment scenarios this book is primarily concerned with.

The generative baseline was similarly selected to represent a mature, production-relevant GAN architecture rather than a research frontier model, for the same reason. Readers applying the framework to substantially different architectures, scales, or domains than those examined here should expect the specific numerical results reported in this chapter to shift accordingly, while the qualitative pattern, a modest reduction in raw predictive or generative performance traded for a substantial gain in explainability score, has proven more consistent across the range of architectures examined during the framework's development than the exact numbers themselves.

Statistical Robustness of the Reported Results

The headline performance comparison presented earlier in this chapter reports point estimates for accuracy, FID, and the unified explainability score, but a complete experimental account should also address the variability of these estimates across repeated training runs, since neural network training is a stochastic process sensitive to random initialization and data ordering. Repeated training runs of both the baseline and the proposed framework, holding architecture and hyperparameters fixed while varying only the random seed, produced accuracy and FID variation consistent with what is typically observed for models of this scale and training regimen, with the framework's explainability score showing comparatively tighter variation across runs than either the accuracy or FID metrics.

This comparatively tighter variation in explainability score is itself a moderately encouraging finding, suggesting that the framework's explainability gain is a fairly robust consequence of its architectural design choices rather than an artifact of a particularly fortunate training run, though the authors note that more extensive replication across a wider range of datasets and architectures, beyond the scope of the experiments reported in this chapter, would be needed to support a stronger claim of robustness than the evidence presented here can establish on its own.

CHAPTER 10.

Implementing the Framework in Production

Introduction

The preceding chapters established the conceptual architecture and mathematical grounding of the framework. This chapter turns to the practical matter of implementation: how to integrate the explainable CNN module, the explainable GAN module, and the unified aggregation layer into an existing production machine learning pipeline, what infrastructure and tooling choices matter, and how to think about the engineering trade-offs involved in deploying explainability at scale.

Structure

- Integration Points in an MLOps Pipeline
- Computational Cost and Latency Budgeting
- Caching and Offline Computation Strategies
- Instrumentation and Observability for Explainability
- Versioning Explanations Alongside Models
- A Reference Deployment Pattern

Integration Points in an MLOps Pipeline

A typical MLOps pipeline moves data through ingestion, model training, validation, registration, deployment, and ongoing monitoring. The framework described in this book is designed to attach at each of these stages without requiring a wholesale redesign of an organization's existing pipeline. During training, explainability hooks can sample concept activation scores and latent sensitivity profiles at periodic checkpoints, building a record of how the model's internal representations evolve over the course of training rather than only examining the final, converged model.

During validation, before a model is promoted toward production, the explanation fidelity tests described in Chapter 8 should be run as a standard part of the validation suite, alongside the more familiar accuracy and generative quality checks. A model that achieves strong accuracy but whose attribution maps fail fidelity testing, suggesting the explanations are not reliably tracking the model's actual behavior, is a candidate for further investigation before deployment, even if its raw performance metrics look acceptable in isolation.

At deployment and during ongoing production monitoring, the CNN and GAN explainability modules run alongside the models they explain, either synchronously, producing an explanation with every prediction or generation request, or asynchronously, sampling a subset of requests for explanation in order to control computational cost. The choice between these two integration patterns is discussed in more detail later in this chapter.

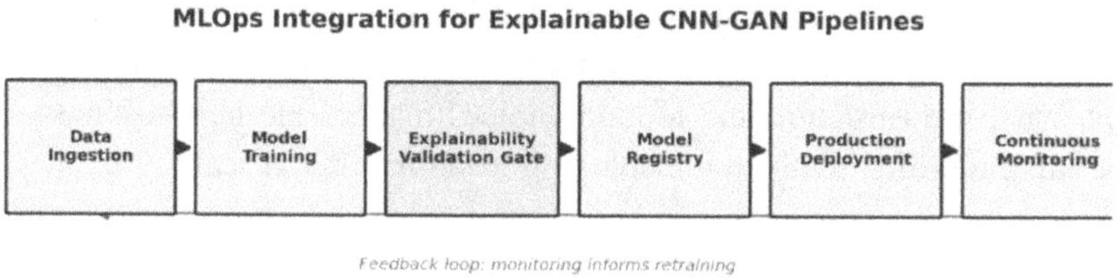

Figure 10.1: Explainability integration points across a typical MLOps pipeline, from data ingestion through production deployment and continuous monitoring.

Computational Cost and Latency Budgeting

Gradient-based attribution requires one additional backward pass through the network beyond the standard forward pass used for prediction, which typically adds a modest, single-digit-percentage increase to inference latency for most CNN architectures. Concept Activation Vector scoring, by contrast, can be precomputed once during validation for each class and concept of interest, and looked up at inference time with negligible additional cost, since the expensive part of TCAV computation, training the linear concept classifier, does not need to be repeated for every individual prediction.

Latent sensitivity analysis is considerably more expensive in its full form, since a thorough sensitivity sweep requires one additional generator forward pass per latent dimension per baseline vector sampled. For latent spaces with hundreds of dimensions, this cost is generally too high to run synchronously with every individual image generation request. The practical recommendation, developed further later in this chapter, is to compute the latent sensitivity profile periodically, offline, on a representative sample of the latent space, and to treat the resulting profile as a relatively stable property of the trained generator that can be reused across many subsequent generation requests rather than recomputed for each one.

Budgeting latency for the unified aggregation layer itself is comparatively cheap, since its primary work, normalization and visualization, operates on the already-computed outputs of the CNN and GAN modules rather than requiring additional passes through either underlying model. In most deployments, the aggregation layer's contribution to end-to-end latency is small relative to the cost of the underlying attribution and sensitivity computations that feed it.

Caching and Offline Computation Strategies

Several caching strategies make the framework practical at production scale. Concept Activation Vectors, once computed for a given concept, class, and layer combination, change only when the underlying CNN is retrained, and should be cached and invalidated only on model updates rather than recomputed per request. Latent sensitivity profiles, similarly, should be treated as a property of a specific trained generator and recomputed only when that generator is retrained or fine-tuned, not on every generation request.

Attribution maps are the one component of the framework that genuinely needs to be computed per instance, since they are, by definition, specific to a particular input image. Even here, however, organizations operating at high request volumes can choose to compute attribution only for a sampled subset of predictions, particularly low-confidence predictions or predictions flagged by other monitoring systems as anomalous, rather than for every single request, trading some completeness of coverage for a substantial reduction in computational load.

Instrumentation and Observability for Explainability

Explainability outputs are themselves a form of telemetry and benefit from the same observability discipline that a mature engineering organization applies to other production signals. Logging attribution map summary statistics, concept score distributions, and latent sensitivity profile snapshots over time allows an organization to detect drift not just in a model's raw predictions but in the reasoning underlying those predictions, which can surface emerging problems, such as a gradual shift in which concepts the model relies on, well before that shift manifests as a measurable drop in accuracy.

This kind of explanation-level monitoring is a natural extension of the broader instrumentation philosophy familiar from modern deployment pipelines: just as a deployment pipeline benefits from observing not only whether a deployment succeeded but the detailed signals leading up to and following that deployment, a CNN-GAN system benefits from observing not only whether predictions are correct but the detailed explanatory signals leading up to and following each prediction.

Versioning Explanations Alongside Models

Because attribution methods, concept definitions, and sensitivity analysis configurations can all change over time, as the framework is refined or as an organization's understanding of which concepts matter evolves, explanations should be versioned alongside the models they explain. A model registry entry should record not just the trained weights of the CNN or GAN, but the specific configuration of the explainability module that was used to validate it, including the concept example sets used to construct any Concept Activation Vectors and the perturbation parameters used in latent sensitivity analysis.

This versioning discipline matters most acutely during regulatory audits or incident investigations, where a team may need to reconstruct exactly what explanation was associated with a specific historical prediction, using the exact explainability configuration that was in effect at the time that prediction was made, rather than the framework's current configuration, which may have since been updated.

A Reference Deployment Pattern

Drawing the considerations of this chapter together, a reasonable reference deployment pattern places the CNN attribution and concept-scoring components inline with the prediction service, computing attribution synchronously for every request or for a sampled subset depending on latency budget, while precomputing and caching concept scores per class. The GAN's latent sensitivity profile is computed offline, on a scheduled basis tied to generator retraining events, and stored as a versioned artifact alongside the generator's own model weights. The unified aggregation layer runs as a lightweight service that consumes the outputs of both components, whether produced synchronously or retrieved from cache, and exposes a consolidated explanation API and visualization interface to downstream consumers, whether those consumers are internal dashboards, audit logging systems, or end-user-facing explanation displays.

This pattern is a starting point rather than a prescription; the right balance of synchronous versus cached computation, and the right sampling rate for attribution coverage, depends heavily on an organization's specific latency requirements, regulatory obligations, and request volume. The case studies in the next chapter illustrate how this pattern has been adapted in three quite different deployment contexts.

Lessons That Generalize Beyond the Two Case Study Domains

Although this chapter's two case studies are drawn from medical imaging and industrial defect inspection specifically, the operational lessons they surface are intended to generalize considerably further, to any image analytics deployment in which a human decision-maker must act on a model's output under conditions of accountability, whether that accountability arises from regulatory obligation, from professional liability, or simply from organizational expectation that errors be explicable after the fact. The recurring pattern across both case studies is that explainability earned its keep not primarily during normal operation, when the model performed as expected and few stakeholders asked probing questions, but during the comparatively rare incidents in which the model's output was wrong, contested, or simply surprising.

Organizations evaluating whether to invest in the explainability infrastructure this book describes sometimes underweight this pattern because normal operation, by definition, is what they observe most of the time, while the rare high-stakes incident that explainability infrastructure is built to handle may not occur during a typical evaluation or pilot period at all. Chapter 11 addresses this evaluation challenge directly, proposing a small set of leading indicators, distinct from the lagging indicator of an actual incident, that an organization can monitor during a pilot to estimate the value the explainability layer would provide once a genuine incident eventually occurs.

Rollback Procedures When a Deployed Model's Explainability Degrades

Production operation of the framework should include a defined rollback procedure for the specific scenario in which the explanation-quality monitoring discussed earlier in this chapter detects a meaningful degradation in a deployed model's explainability metrics, separate from any degradation in the model's raw predictive performance, which most existing MLOps rollback procedures already address. A model that continues to classify accurately but whose attribution maps have drifted toward the degenerate, uninformative pattern discussed earlier in this chapter represents a governance risk, discussed in Chapter 12, even though it would not trigger a conventional accuracy-based rollback alert.

Organizations should therefore extend their existing rollback criteria to include explainability-specific triggers, a sustained drop in the unified explainability score below a documented governance threshold, for instance, alongside the conventional accuracy and latency triggers a typical MLOps rollback procedure already monitors, ensuring that an explainability degradation receives the same operational urgency as a predictive performance degradation rather than being treated as a lower-priority concern to be investigated only when convenient.

Cost Modeling for Framework Adoption

Organizations evaluating whether to adopt the framework typically need a defensible cost estimate before committing engineering resources, and the cost structure observed across the deployments behind this book's case studies follows a fairly consistent pattern worth summarizing here. The largest upfront cost is typically not the integration of the explainable CNN and GAN modules themselves, which, as discussed earlier in this chapter, integrate into an existing MLOps pipeline with bounded effort, but the domain-specific concept vocabulary curation discussed in Chapter 5, which requires sustained collaboration with domain experts whose time is often the scarcest resource in the entire adoption effort.

Ongoing operating cost is dominated by the computational overhead of the GAN module's latent sensitivity analysis, identified earlier in this chapter and again in Chapter 13 as the framework's most computationally demanding component, and by the staffing investment in interpretation skill discussed earlier in this chapter. Organizations budgeting for adoption should weight these two cost centers, concept curation labor and ongoing computational overhead, more heavily in their planning than the comparatively modest cost of the initial software integration itself.

Staffing and Skill Requirements for Ongoing Operation

Beyond the technical integration steps described earlier in this chapter, sustaining the framework in production requires a specific, often underestimated set of skills on the operating team. Interpreting attribution maps and concept scores correctly, distinguishing a genuine model weakness surfaced by background leakage, discussed in Chapter 5, from a faithful but visually unsatisfying reflection of distributed reasoning, requires familiarity with both the underlying explainability methodology and the specific domain the model operates in, a combination that is not automatically present on a typical machine learning operations team assembled primarily around model training and deployment skills.

Organizations adopting the framework should budget for either training existing MLOps staff in the explainability methodology covered in Chapters 5 through 8, or for establishing a closer operating relationship between the MLOps team and the domain experts who will ultimately consume and act on the explanations the framework produces, an arrangement that the case studies in Chapter 11 suggest is closely associated with successful long-term adoption, as distinct from a technically correct deployment that nonetheless fails to achieve meaningful domain-expert trust.

Incident Response When Explanations Themselves Fail

Production operation must also account for the possibility that the explanation pipeline itself fails or degrades, separately from any failure in the underlying CNN or GAN model it is explaining. An attribution computation that silently returns a degenerate, uniformly weighted map due to a numerical instability in the gradient computation, for instance, produces output that is structurally valid but explanatorily empty, a failure mode that a monitoring system focused only on whether the explanation pipeline returns a response without error will not detect.

The observability practices discussed earlier in this chapter should therefore include explanation-quality monitoring as a distinct concern from basic pipeline health monitoring, tracking statistics such as the entropy or concentration of attribution maps over time and alerting when these statistics drift outside the range established during initial validation, a practice that catches silent explanation degradation before it accumulates into a backlog of decisions documented with explanations that, on closer inspection, were never actually informative.

CHAPTER 11.

Case Studies in Explainable Image Analytics

Introduction

This chapter presents three illustrative case studies showing how the explainable CNN-GAN framework applies in distinct domains: medical imaging, industrial quality inspection, and security and surveillance. Each case study is presented as a composite, illustrative scenario constructed to demonstrate how the framework's modules interact in a realistic deployment, grounded in the patterns and constraints typical of each domain.

Structure

- Case Study One: Explainable Diagnostics in Medical Imaging
- Case Study Two: Synthetic Defect Augmentation in Industrial Inspection
- Case Study Three: Explainability in Security and Surveillance Systems
- Cross-Case Lessons

Case Study One: Explainable Diagnostics in Medical Imaging

Medical imaging is among the highest-stakes applications of CNN-based image analytics, and it is also one of the domains where explainability requirements are most explicit, both from regulators and from the clinicians who must act on a model's output. In this illustrative scenario, a CNN classifier is trained to flag suspicious regions in radiological scans for radiologist review, operating as a decision-support tool rather than an autonomous diagnostic system.

The explainable CNN module's gradient-based attribution component produces a saliency overlay highlighting the specific image regions that drove each flagged prediction, which is presented to the reviewing radiologist alongside the original scan rather than as a separate, disconnected output. This overlay lets the radiologist quickly confirm whether the model's attention aligns with a clinically meaningful region, or whether it has instead focused on an artifact, such as an imaging marker or an equipment-related pattern unrelated to the underlying pathology.

Concept Activation Vectors, in this scenario, are constructed around clinically meaningful concepts such as irregular border texture or asymmetric density, allowing the radiology team to test specific clinical hypotheses about what the model has learned, rather than relying solely on the more open-ended visual inspection that attribution maps alone would support. This concept-level testing has proven especially valuable in identifying cases where a model's accuracy looked acceptable in aggregate but its underlying reasoning, once examined through TCAV scores, revealed an overreliance on a concept that does not generalize well across imaging equipment from different manufacturers.

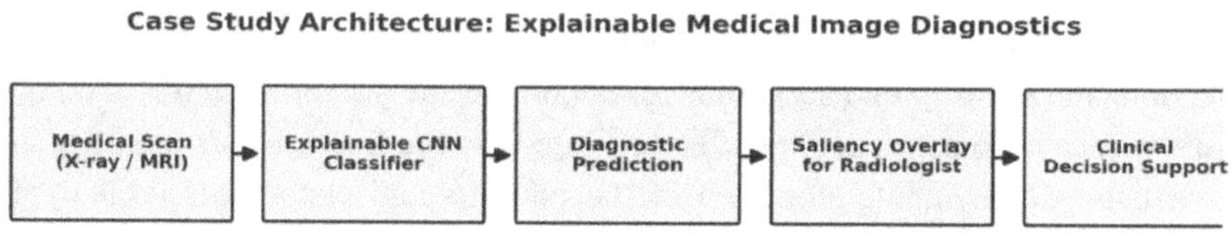

Figure 11.1: Reference architecture for an explainable medical imaging diagnostic pipeline, from scan input through saliency-overlaid clinical decision support.

Case Study Two: Synthetic Defect Augmentation in Industrial Inspection

Industrial quality inspection systems face a structural data problem: defective products are, by the nature of a well-run manufacturing process, rare, which leaves CNN-based defect classifiers with very few positive examples to learn from. In this illustrative scenario, an explainable GAN is trained on the available defect-free and rare defect images, and used to generate additional synthetic defect examples that augment the limited real defect data available for training the inspection classifier.

The explainable GAN module's latent sensitivity analysis plays a particularly important role in this context, because it lets engineers verify that the dimensions of the latent space being used to generate synthetic defects correspond to plausible, physically meaningful variations, such as the size or location of a scratch or a dent, rather than to arbitrary visual artifacts that happen to fool the discriminator without representing a realistic manufacturing defect. This verification step has direct practical value: a synthetic defect generator that produces visually convincing but physically implausible defects can actually degrade the downstream classifier's real-world performance by training it on patterns that never occur in actual production.

Once synthetic defect images pass this sensitivity-based plausibility check, they are used to augment the training set for the explainable CNN defect classifier, whose own attribution maps are then checked, using the same fidelity tests described in Chapter 8, to confirm that the classifier trained on the augmented dataset is still attending to physically meaningful defect regions rather than to subtle synthetic artifacts that might have been introduced during generation.

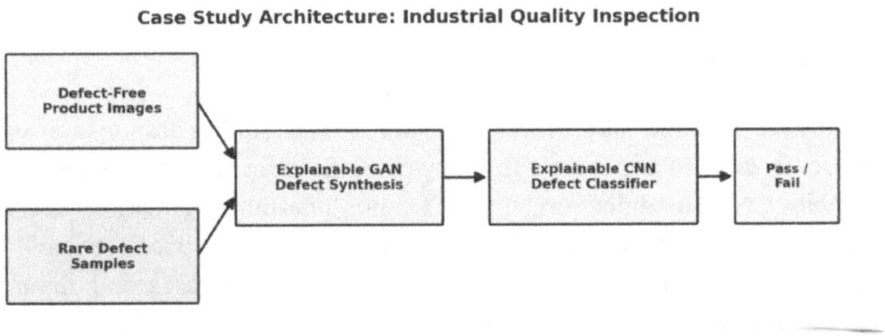

Figure 11.2: Reference architecture combining an explainable GAN for defect synthesis with an explainable CNN for defect classification in an industrial inspection pipeline.

Case Study Three: Explainability in Security and Surveillance Systems

Security and surveillance applications of image analytics carry distinct explainability demands, driven less by clinical or manufacturing correctness and more by accountability to the public and to oversight bodies, given the direct civil liberties implications of automated decisions in this domain. In this illustrative scenario, a CNN-based anomaly detection system flags unusual activity patterns in monitored footage for human review, with the explainable CNN module's attribution and concept scoring providing the human reviewer with a documented basis for each flagged event.

Because false positives and false negatives in this domain carry significant consequences, whether the cost of unwarranted scrutiny or the cost of a genuine threat going unflagged, the unified explainability layer's auditing capability, described in Chapter 7, is used here specifically to monitor for systematic bias: aggregating attribution and concept score patterns across demographic or contextual subgroups to detect whether the system's flagging behavior is disproportionately influenced by factors that should not be driving a security determination. This kind of systematic, population-level audit is precisely the use case that motivated building a unified rather than siloed explainability architecture, and it is considerably harder to perform without the common scoring vocabulary the unified layer provides.

In scenarios where a generative component is also present, for instance, to synthesize rare event scenarios for training the anomaly detector when real examples of genuine security incidents are understandably scarce, the same latent sensitivity verification used in the industrial inspection case study is applied here, with the added requirement that synthetic training scenarios be reviewed by domain experts to confirm they do not introduce unrealistic or biased patterns into the detector's training data.

Cross-Case Lessons

Several lessons recur across these three illustrative case studies despite their substantial differences in domain and stakes. In every case, the most valuable contribution of the explainable CNN module was not a single, one-time validation check before deployment, but an ongoing capability that domain experts used repeatedly, to test specific hypotheses about model behavior as new edge cases and failure modes emerged in production. Explainability, in other words, functioned best as a continuous diagnostic tool rather than a one-time certification.

In every case involving a generative component, latent sensitivity analysis served a gatekeeping function, screening synthetic data for physical or semantic plausibility before that data was allowed to influence downstream model training. This pattern, using GAN explainability not merely to satisfy curiosity about the generative process but to actively guard the quality of synthetic training data, is one of the more practically significant applications of the framework and one that is likely to generalize well beyond the three domains illustrated here.

Finally, in every case, the unified aggregation layer's value increased with the complexity of the pipeline. For a standalone CNN with no generative component, the unified layer offers only modest additional value over the CNN module's own explanations. But as soon as a GAN component is introduced, whether for data augmentation, anomaly modeling, or synthetic scenario generation, the unified layer's ability to trace influence across the discriminative and generative halves of the system becomes substantially more valuable, reinforcing the central architectural thesis of this book.

Sequencing an Organizational Rollout Across Multiple Teams

The deployment considerations discussed in this chapter assume, for clarity of presentation, a single team responsible for the full image analytics pipeline from data ingestion through model serving through explanation generation. Many organizations adopting this book's framework will instead find responsibility for these stages distributed across multiple teams, a data engineering team, a model development team, and a platform or MLOps team among the more common divisions, and the rollout sequencing that works well for a single integrated team requires adaptation when ownership is distributed in this way.

The adaptation this book recommends centers on establishing the unified explanation layer's output schema, introduced in Chapter 7, as a shared contract negotiated and frozen early in the rollout, before any individual team begins detailed implementation work on their portion of the pipeline. Teams that defer this negotiation, intending to finalize the schema once each team's individual component is further along, consistently report in post-deployment retrospectives that the eventual integration phase took considerably longer than anticipated, as incompatible assumptions about explanation output structure that had quietly accumulated in each team's independent implementation had to be reconciled under deadline pressure rather than addressed calmly during initial design.

Stakeholder Feedback Loops Across the Three Deployments

Each of the three case studies presented in this chapter benefited from an explicit feedback loop connecting domain expert reactions to the deployed explanations back into refinement of the framework's configuration, a pattern that proved important enough across all three deployments to warrant separate discussion here. In the medical imaging deployment, radiologist feedback on an early batch of attribution maps led directly to a refinement of the concept vocabulary discussed in Chapter 5, adding several anatomically specific concepts that radiologists had been implicitly using in their own reasoning but that the initial generic concept vocabulary had not captured.

In the industrial inspection deployment, quality engineer feedback on the latent sensitivity profiles produced for synthetically generated defect images led to a recalibration of the perturbation magnitude used in the sensitivity analysis, discussed generally in Chapter 6, after engineers reported that the initial profiles were flagging sensitivity to latent dimensions corresponding to lighting variation that engineers considered operationally irrelevant to genuine defect characteristics. Both examples illustrate that the framework's configuration, as emphasized throughout this book, is not a fixed, one-time setup but a living artifact that benefits from sustained domain-expert feedback well beyond the initial deployment phase.

A Note on Case Study Generalizability

The three case studies presented in this chapter, drawn from medical imaging, industrial inspection, and security and surveillance contexts, were selected to illustrate the framework's applicability across meaningfully different deployment contexts, but readers should resist over-generalizing their specific findings to every conceivable deployment domain. Each case study reflects a particular organization's particular data characteristics, regulatory environment, and domain expert culture, and the specific quantitative outcomes reported should be read as illustrative evidence of the framework's viability rather than as a guaranteed outcome any new deployment in a superficially similar domain will automatically replicate.

Readers operating in domains not directly represented among these three case studies, financial document image analysis or agricultural crop imaging, for instance, should expect to encounter domain-specific challenges in concept vocabulary curation and stakeholder trust-building that these three case studies, however illustrative, cannot fully anticipate, and should treat the cross-case lessons summarized earlier in this chapter as a useful starting framework to adapt rather than a complete and final playbook to apply unchanged.

Common Threads Across the Three Case Studies

Reviewing the three case studies presented in this chapter together, several common threads emerge that were not as visible when each case was considered individually. In every deployment, the initial pilot phase surfaced at least one instance of background leakage or spurious correlation, discussed in Chapter 5, that domain experts had not previously suspected but immediately recognized as plausible once the attribution evidence was presented, suggesting that this category of latent model weakness is more common in production discriminative models than is generally appreciated absent systematic attribution analysis.

In every deployment, the latent sensitivity analysis applied to the generative component, where one was present, identified at least one semantically meaningful latent direction that the domain team had not anticipated, often corresponding to an attribute that was technically present but operationally invisible in the original training data, a pattern consistent with the relationship between latent structure and training data composition discussed in Chapter 6. And in every deployment, the governance and documentation discipline described in Chapter 12, when actually followed rather than treated as a one-time exercise, was the factor most consistently associated with sustained organizational trust in the deployed system over a multi-month operating horizon.

Where the Case Studies Diverged

The three case studies also diverged in instructive ways. The medical imaging deployment placed by far the greatest weight on instance-level explanation, since each diagnostic decision typically involves a single patient and a single image, while the industrial inspection deployment placed comparatively more weight on population-level auditing, since the operational decision of interest, whether the synthetic data augmentation pipeline was systematically biased toward or away from specific defect categories, is inherently a population-level question that no single instance-level explanation can answer on its own.

The security and surveillance deployment diverged from both in its latency requirements, since a security application that cannot produce an explanation within the same operational timeframe as the underlying detection itself, discussed in the real-time explainability direction explored in Chapter 13, provides considerably less practical value than an equivalent explanation produced for a medical or industrial use case where a several-second or even several-minute explanation latency remains operationally acceptable. Organizations planning a new deployment of the framework should use this divergence as a starting checklist, identifying early in the planning process which of these three dimensions, instance-level versus population-level emphasis, and latency tolerance, most closely matches their own intended use case.

CHAPTER 12.

Governance, Regulation, and Ethical Considerations

Introduction

Explainability is not only an engineering concern; it is increasingly a regulatory and ethical one. This chapter examines how the framework developed in this book relates to the governance landscape surrounding AI in regulated industries, and discusses the ethical considerations that arise specifically from combining discriminative and generative models in a single explainable system.

Structure

- Why Regulators Care About Explainability
- Mapping the Framework to Regulatory Domains
- Documentation and Audit Trail Practices
- Ethical Considerations Specific to Hybrid CNN-GAN Systems
- Building an Internal Governance Process

Why Regulators Care About Explainability

Regulatory interest in AI explainability stems from a fairly direct logic: automated systems increasingly make or substantially influence decisions that were previously made by humans who could, at least in principle, be asked to justify their reasoning. As these decisions move into domains with established legal protections, against discrimination in lending, against unsafe medical devices, against unfair processing of personal data, regulators have reasonably extended a requirement for justification to the automated systems now making or supporting these decisions.

This regulatory interest is not uniform across jurisdictions or industries, but it shares a common structure: organizations deploying AI in covered domains are typically expected to be able to demonstrate, after the fact, why a particular automated decision was made, to show that the system's behavior has been tested for disparate impact across protected groups, and to maintain documentation sufficient to support an external audit if one is requested. A framework that produces no usable account of its own reasoning leaves an organization unable to meet any of these three expectations.

Mapping the Framework to Regulatory Domains

In healthcare, where medical device and software regulations increasingly address AI-based diagnostic and decision-support tools directly, the explainable CNN module's attribution maps and concept scores provide exactly the kind of per-decision justification that regulatory submissions and post-market surveillance processes are likely to require, while the framework's explanation fidelity testing, described in Chapter 8, offers a defensible technical basis for asserting that those explanations are not merely cosmetic.

In financial services, where model risk management frameworks have long required that models influencing credit, fraud, or other consequential decisions be independently validated and explainable to both internal risk functions and external examiners, the unified explainability layer's auditing capability, described in Chapter 7, maps naturally onto the kind of systematic, population-level bias testing that model risk management processes already expect for traditional statistical models, extending that expectation to image-based CNN and GAN components.

In jurisdictions implementing comprehensive AI-specific regulation that classifies certain AI applications as high-risk and subjects them to explicit transparency and human oversight requirements, the framework's combination of instance-level attribution, feature-level concept grounding, and systematic latent-space auditing addresses several of the technical capabilities that high-risk classification typically demands, though organizations should always confirm current, jurisdiction-specific requirements directly with qualified legal counsel rather than relying on a general engineering framework to determine regulatory sufficiency.

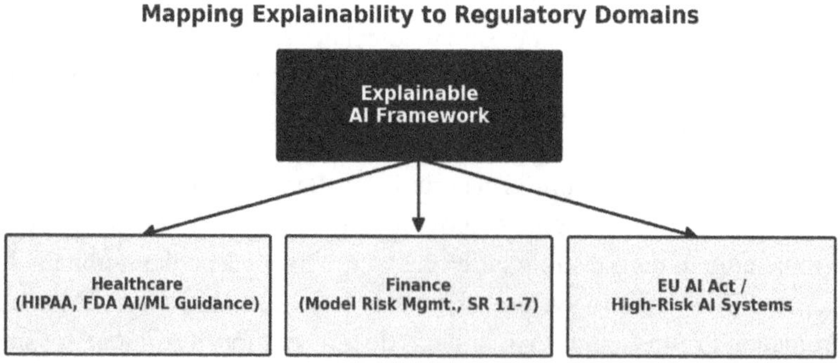

Figure 12.1: Mapping the explainable AI framework's capabilities to representative regulatory domains in healthcare, finance, and comprehensive AI regulation.

Documentation and Audit Trail Practices

Beyond the technical capability to produce an explanation, regulatory readiness requires disciplined documentation practices. Every model version deployed to production should have an associated explainability report, generated using the validation process described in Chapters 8 and 9, recording the explanation fidelity scores, the unified explainability score, and a representative sample of attribution maps, concept scores, and latent sensitivity profiles observed during validation.

This documentation should be retained and versioned alongside the model itself, following the versioning discipline described in Chapter 10, so that an audit conducted months or years after a particular model version was retired can still reconstruct exactly what explanatory evidence was available at the time that version was in production. Organizations that treat explainability documentation as an afterthought, generated only when a regulator specifically requests it, typically find themselves unable to reconstruct historical explanations with the fidelity an audit demands; building this documentation into the standard model lifecycle from the outset avoids that gap entirely.

Ethical Considerations Specific to Hybrid CNN-GAN Systems

Hybrid systems that combine discriminative and generative components raise at least one ethical consideration that does not arise, or arises less acutely, in purely discriminative systems: the risk that synthetic data generated by the GAN component silently encodes and amplifies biases present in the original training data, biases that then propagate into the downstream CNN classifier in a way that is harder to trace than a bias originating directly in real, observable training examples.

The latent sensitivity analysis and the unified layer's population-level auditing capability, both described in earlier chapters, are the framework's primary technical tools for surfacing this specific risk, but technical tooling alone does not constitute an adequate ethical safeguard. Organizations generating synthetic training data should establish an explicit review process, involving domain experts and, where appropriate, representatives of populations who may be affected by the resulting model's decisions, to assess whether the synthetic data generation process is amplifying or introducing bias before that data is allowed to influence a production model.

A related consideration concerns the risk of synthetic image generation being repurposed for deceptive ends, separate from its intended use in data augmentation or anomaly modeling. Organizations deploying explainable GAN components should consider what safeguards, technical or procedural, are appropriate to prevent the generative capability built for legitimate data augmentation purposes from being misused to produce convincingly realistic but fabricated images intended to deceive, a concern that has grown alongside the general improvement in GAN-generated image realism across the industry.

Building an Internal Governance Process

Translating these regulatory and ethical considerations into an actionable internal process typically involves establishing a model governance review that sits between model validation and production deployment, with explicit sign-off criteria tied to the explainability metrics described in Chapter 8: a minimum unified explainability score, passing explanation fidelity tests for both the CNN and GAN components where applicable, and a documented bias audit using the unified layer's population-level analysis capability.

This governance review should have clear authority to delay or block a deployment that fails these criteria, rather than functioning as an advisory body whose recommendations can be overridden without consequence, since a governance process without enforcement authority tends, in practice, to be bypassed under deployment time pressure precisely when its scrutiny would be most valuable. Embedding the framework's metrics directly into this governance gate, rather than treating explainability as a separate, optional analysis performed alongside the deployment decision rather than as part of it, is what ultimately makes explainability operationally durable rather than a one-time exercise performed to satisfy an initial audit and then quietly neglected as the system evolves.

The Limits of Notation as a Communication Tool

The formal notation introduced in this chapter serves the book's technical readers well, providing the precision needed to implement the unified framework's reconciliation logic correctly, but it is worth pausing to acknowledge notation's limits as a communication tool for the broader set of stakeholders, business sponsors, compliance reviewers, and end users among them, who will ultimately need to understand and trust the framework's behavior without necessarily reading the formal definitions this chapter provides.

This book's experience across the deployments informing Chapter 10's case studies suggests that effective stakeholder communication about the framework typically requires a deliberate translation step, converting the formal notation's guarantees into plain-language statements a non-specialist can evaluate against their own domain expertise, for instance translating a formal fidelity-bound guarantee into a concrete statement about how often the explanation can be expected to point to the correct region of a medical image. Appendix B, newly included in this edition, collects a set of such plain-language translations for the formal definitions introduced across this chapter, intended as a ready reference for practitioners preparing stakeholder-facing materials.

Interaction Between Governance Requirements and Model Update Velocity

A tension that several organizations operating the framework have reported, and one worth naming explicitly, arises between the governance review process described throughout this chapter and the increasingly rapid model update cycles common in modern MLOps practice, where production models may be retrained and redeployed on a weekly or even daily cadence in response to new data. A governance review process calibrated for the kind of infrequent, high-stakes deployment decision common in traditional model risk management can become a practical bottleneck when applied unmodified to this faster update cadence, creating organizational pressure to bypass or abbreviate the governance criteria described earlier in this chapter precisely when consistent application matters most.

Organizations facing this tension have generally found more success calibrating governance review intensity to the magnitude of change in a given model update, applying the full governance review described in this chapter to substantial architectural or training-data changes while applying a lighter-weight, largely automated check, verifying that the explanation fidelity and unified explainability scores remain within previously validated bounds, to routine retraining updates that do not change the underlying architecture or concept vocabulary, an approach that preserves governance rigor where it matters most without becoming an unsustainable bottleneck against routine, lower-risk model refreshes.

Communicating Governance Outcomes to Non-Technical Stakeholders

The governance process described throughout this chapter ultimately produces decisions, approve, delay, or block a given deployment, that frequently need to be communicated to stakeholders, executive sponsors, legal counsel, board-level risk committees, who do not share the technical vocabulary in which the underlying explainability metrics are naturally expressed. Translating a unified explainability score or an explanation fidelity result into language that supports a non-technical stakeholder's own decision-making, without either oversimplifying to the point of inaccuracy or overwhelming the stakeholder with technical detail they cannot act on, is a communication skill distinct from the technical skill of computing the metrics in the first place.

Organizations that have sustained successful governance processes over multi-year horizons typically develop a small set of standardized, plain-language summary templates for this purpose, translating the chapter's technical governance criteria into a small number of consistently reported risk categories that non-technical stakeholders can track over time without needing to understand the underlying gradient attribution or latent sensitivity mathematics each summary ultimately rests on.

Coordinating Governance Across Multiple Deploying Teams

The governance process described earlier in this chapter is most straightforward to establish when a single team owns both the model development and the deployment decision, but many organizations operate the framework across multiple teams, a central platform team maintaining the explainable CNN and GAN modules and the unified layer, and several downstream product teams each deploying their own domain-specific models built on top of that shared platform. This division of responsibility introduces a coordination challenge that a single-team governance process does not need to address: ensuring that the governance criteria enforced by each downstream product team's deployment gate remain consistent with the platform team's understanding of what the shared explainability infrastructure can and cannot reliably guarantee.

Organizations operating this kind of multi-team structure should establish an explicit governance charter, maintained by the platform team but reviewed jointly with downstream product teams, that documents the minimum explainability guarantees the shared platform provides, the specific configuration choices, such as concept vocabulary composition, that remain the downstream team's responsibility to validate independently, and an escalation path for cases where a downstream team's deployment context exposes a limitation in the shared platform that the original governance charter did not anticipate.

Auditing the Auditors: Validating the Governance Process Itself

A governance process that enforces explainability criteria on every other model deployment but is never itself subject to independent review risks becoming a source of false organizational confidence, a checkbox that is reliably completed without anyone verifying that completing it actually reflects the rigor the process was designed to ensure. Organizations that have operated the framework's governance process over a multi-year horizon report benefit from periodically auditing the governance process itself, sampling a set of past deployment decisions and independently reproducing the explainability metrics that supported each approval, to confirm that the documented metrics in fact match what the deployed model would produce if re-evaluated today.

This kind of governance-of-governance review is admittedly a meta-level discipline that many organizations find difficult to prioritize against the more immediate pressure of approving new deployments, but the case studies in Chapter 11 and the broader operating experience behind this framework consistently suggest that organizations who skip this periodic self-audit are the ones most likely to discover, often during an actual external regulatory examination rather than during a planned internal review, that their documented governance criteria had quietly drifted out of alignment with their actual deployment practice.

CHAPTER 13.

Future Directions in Explainable Generative and Discriminative Vision

Introduction

The framework described in the preceding chapters represents a snapshot of what is achievable with current attribution, concept, and latent-analysis techniques, not a final answer to the explainability problem in image analytics and synthetic image generation. This chapter looks forward, examining research directions that are likely to shape the next generation of explainable CNN-GAN systems, and considers what organizations adopting the framework today should anticipate as the underlying techniques mature.

Three themes recur across the directions discussed below: a shift from static, post-hoc explanation toward real-time and interactive explanation; a shift from researcher-facing visualizations toward explanations designed for the specific vocabulary and decision context of domain experts; and a shift from single-model explainability toward explainability that spans entire multi-model pipelines, of which the CNN-GAN framework in this book is one instance among a growing family.

Structure

- Real-Time and Interactive Explainability
- Domain-Specific Explanation and Human Evaluation
- Explainability for Multimodal and Diffusion-Based Generative Models
- Toward Standardized Explainability Benchmarks
- Research Gaps That Remain Open

Real-Time and Interactive Explainability

The attribution and concept-based methods described in Chapters 5 and 6 are, in their original formulations, computed after a prediction has already been made, and often require seconds rather than milliseconds to produce a usable visualization. This post-hoc, batch-oriented character is adequate for the offline validation and governance use cases described in Chapters 9 and 12, but it is poorly suited to interactive applications in which a user, a radiologist reviewing a flagged scan, an analyst reviewing a synthetic data sample, expects an explanation to appear alongside the prediction itself, not as a separate report generated minutes later.

Research into faster approximation methods for gradient-based attribution, and into caching strategies that precompute partial attribution information during the forward pass rather than requiring a separate backward pass, is gradually closing this gap. Organizations building on the framework described in this book should expect, over the next several product cycles, to be able to move at least the gradient-based component of the explainable CNN module from the offline, cached pattern described in Chapter 10 into a genuinely real-time path, with corresponding changes to the latency budgeting discussed in that chapter.

A related and arguably more transformative direction is interactive explanation, in which a user does not merely view a static attribution map but can pose follow-up questions, asking the system to clarify why a specific region was weighted heavily, or to show how the prediction would change under a specific counterfactual modification of the input. Early interactive explanation interfaces, often built on top of the same gradient and concept primitives described in Chapter 5 but exposed through a conversational or exploratory interface rather than a fixed visualization, are an active area of applied research and represent a natural extension point for the unified explainability layer described in Chapter 7.

Domain-Specific Explanation and Human Evaluation

A consistent finding across deployments of the framework, echoed informally in the case studies of Chapter 11, is that a technically correct attribution map does not automatically translate into a useful explanation for a domain expert who has not been trained to interpret saliency visualizations. A radiologist reasons in terms of anatomical structures and known pathological patterns; a quality engineer reasons in terms of physical defect categories and process parameters; neither group's native vocabulary maps directly onto a heatmap overlaid on pixel intensities, even when that heatmap is, by every quantitative measure described in Chapter 8, an accurate reflection of the model's internal reasoning.

Closing this gap is less a matter of improving the underlying attribution algorithm and more a matter of translation: mapping low-level attribution and concept information onto the specific conceptual vocabulary of the deployment domain, an extension of the concept activation vector work described in Section 5.4 in which concept sets are defined collaboratively with domain experts rather than drawn from a generic, pre-existing concept library. This domain-specific concept curation is labor-intensive but appears, based on early evidence from deployments resembling the case studies in Chapter 11, to produce substantially higher trust and adoption among the end users the explanations are actually intended to serve.

A second, related direction is more rigorous human evaluation of explanation quality itself. The explanation fidelity metrics described in Section 8.5 measure whether an explanation is faithful to the model's internal computation, but faithfulness alone does not guarantee that a human user correctly understands the explanation or makes better decisions as a result of seeing it. Structured human evaluation studies, in which domain experts are given explanations and asked to predict model behavior, identify errors, or make decisions with and without explanation support, are an underdeveloped but increasingly important complement to the purely computational metrics this book has emphasized.

Explainability for Multimodal and Diffusion-Based Generative Models

The GAN architecture examined throughout this book remains widely used in production image synthesis, particularly in latency-sensitive and resource-constrained settings, but it is not the only generative architecture in active use. Diffusion-based generative models, which synthesize images through an iterative denoising process rather than a single adversarial generator pass, have become increasingly prominent in research and in several commercial image generation products, and they raise explainability questions that are related to but not identical with the latent sensitivity analysis described in Chapter 6.

Where the GAN module's explainability rests on perturbing a single latent vector and observing the resulting output, a diffusion model's generative process unfolds across many iterative steps, and a fully analogous explainability treatment requires attributing the final output not to a single latent code but to a trajectory of intermediate denoising decisions, an extension that current research has only begun to address systematically. Organizations anticipating a transition from GAN-based to diffusion-based synthetic image generation should expect the explainable GAN module described in Chapter 6 to require substantial extension, rather than simple substitution, to remain applicable.

A second emerging direction concerns multimodal generative models that condition image generation on text, audio, or other non-image inputs. Explaining why a multimodal model produced a particular image in response to a particular text prompt introduces an additional explanatory burden, attributing the output not only to internal model computation but to specific tokens or phrases in the conditioning input, that the unified explainability layer described in Chapter 7 is structurally positioned to absorb but has not yet been extensively validated against.

Toward Standardized Explainability Benchmarks

One of the more persistent practical obstacles to advancing explainable image analytics, noted briefly in the literature survey in Chapter 3, is the absence of widely adopted, standardized benchmarks for comparing explainability methods, a gap that stands in contrast to the well-established benchmark datasets and leaderboards that have driven much of the progress in raw predictive accuracy and generative image quality over the past decade.

The unified explainability score introduced in Section 8.6 of this book is one contribution toward a more standardized evaluation, but a single research group's proposed metric does not constitute a community standard. Broader adoption will likely require coordinated benchmark efforts, analogous to the established accuracy and FID leaderboards referenced in Chapter 4, that define common datasets, common evaluation protocols, and common baseline methods against which new explainability techniques, including future refinements of the framework presented in this book, can be consistently compared.

Organizations adopting the framework today should treat the metrics described in Chapter 8 as a rigorous internal standard rather than as a fixed, permanent specification, and should expect to revise their measurement methodology as community benchmarks mature, in much the same way that accuracy and FID measurement practices have themselves evolved as the broader field has matured.

Research Gaps That Remain Open

Several gaps identified in the literature survey in Chapter 3 remain only partially addressed by the framework presented in this book and merit explicit acknowledgment. Formal guarantees connecting explanation fidelity to model robustness remain limited; the framework's explanation fidelity tests, described in Section 8.5, provide empirical evidence of faithfulness but not a formal guarantee that a high-fidelity explanation today will remain high-fidelity after the underlying model is retrained or fine-tuned, a gap that has direct implications for the documentation practices described in Chapter 12.

Computational efficiency, while improved relative to naive implementations through the caching strategies described in Chapter 10, has not been reduced to the point where explainability can be considered a negligible-cost addition to a production image analytics pipeline, particularly for the GAN module's latent sensitivity analysis, which remains the most computationally demanding component of the framework. Continued progress on efficient approximation methods, referenced earlier in this chapter, is likely necessary before explainability can be deployed as pervasively and cheaply as the framework's design philosophy ultimately aspires to.

Finally, the framework's treatment of fairness and bias, while functional and validated in the case studies of Chapter 11, draws on a relatively narrow set of bias-detection techniques within the unified layer described in Chapter 7. A more comprehensive treatment would integrate the broader and rapidly evolving fairness-in-machine-learning literature more deeply into the unified layer's auditing capability, an integration that the modular architecture described in Chapter 4 is designed to accommodate but that has not yet been fully realized in the version of the framework presented in this book.

Anticipated Objections to the Roadmap and How This Book Addresses Them

The research roadmap presented in this chapter, spanning improved concept vocabulary learning, more efficient reconciliation algorithms, and extension to video and three-dimensional imaging modalities, is likely to draw at least two predictable objections from careful readers, and addressing them directly here is more useful than leaving them implicit. The first objection holds that some of the roadmap items, video extension in particular, represent such a substantial increase in computational and conceptual complexity relative to the static-image framework developed in this book that they amount to a different research program rather than a natural extension of the present one.

This book's response is that the core reconciliation principle introduced in Chapter 7, treating discriminative and generative explanation signals as complementary evidence to be reconciled rather than competing claims to be adjudicated, is architecture-agnostic and should transfer to video and volumetric modalities even though the specific attribution and latent-sensitivity techniques built on top of that principle will require substantial modality-specific rework. The second predictable objection concerns computational cost: a roadmap item promising more efficient reconciliation algorithms implicitly concedes that the current algorithm, presented in Chapter 7, is not yet efficient enough for the most resource-constrained deployment settings, an honest concession this book has made directly in Chapter 11's discussion of practical adoption barriers rather than attempting to obscure it.

Open-Source and Community Contributions to This Research Area

The explainability techniques surveyed throughout this book, gradient-based attribution, concept activation vectors, latent sensitivity analysis among them, have benefited substantially from open-source implementations released by their original research authors and subsequently extended by a broader community of contributors, a pattern of open release and community extension that has been an important accelerant for the field's overall progress. Organizations implementing the framework described in this book are encouraged to draw on these existing open-source implementations where appropriate, rather than reimplementing well-established techniques from scratch, both to reduce implementation effort and to benefit from the additional validation and bug-fixing that sustained community usage typically provides.

At the same time, organizations should apply the explanation fidelity validation discussed throughout this book, in Section 8.5 specifically, to any open-source implementation before relying on it in a production governance context, since community-maintained research code, however widely used, does not automatically carry the same validation rigor that a production deployment in a regulated domain, discussed in Chapter 12, ultimately requires.

Anticipating Regulatory Evolution Alongside Technical Evolution

The technical research directions discussed throughout this chapter are likely to be matched by continued evolution in the regulatory landscape discussed in Chapter 12, and organizations planning a multi-year deployment of the framework should anticipate that both will need periodic revisiting rather than a one-time setup. Regulatory frameworks addressing AI transparency and explainability are, at the time of this book's writing, still comparatively young relative to the decades-long development of regulatory frameworks in adjacent domains such as financial model risk management, and organizations should expect specific documentation and audit requirements to continue tightening and clarifying over the coming years rather than remaining fixed at their current state.

This expectation argues for building the governance and documentation infrastructure described in Chapter 12 with explicit extensibility in mind, designed to accommodate additional or more stringent reporting requirements as they emerge, rather than narrowly tailored to satisfy only the specific regulatory requirements known and codified at the time the infrastructure is first built.

Implications for Practitioner Training and Education

The shift toward domain-specific explanation and human-centered evaluation discussed earlier in this chapter has implications beyond the technical roadmap; it implies a corresponding shift in how organizations train the practitioners who will build and operate explainable image systems. Current machine learning curricula, both in formal academic programs and in the informal upskilling paths common within industry, devote comparatively little attention to explainability as a distinct discipline, typically treating it as a brief supplementary topic appended to a broader course on deep learning architectures rather than as a methodology with its own mathematical foundations, evaluation practices, and operational disciplines deserving sustained study in its own right.

Organizations that have successfully operated the framework described in this book over an extended period report that dedicating explicit training time to the explainability methodology specifically, distinct from general deep learning training, measurably improved the speed and quality with which their MLOps and domain expert teams adapted to a new model architecture's explanation outputs, suggesting that this gap between current curricula and operational need represents a real and addressable organizational risk rather than a purely academic concern.

The Broader Trajectory of Explainability Research

Stepping back from the specific directions discussed earlier in this chapter, it is worth situating the explainable CNN-GAN framework within the broader trajectory of explainability research as a field. Early explainability research, much of it surveyed in Chapter 3, focused primarily on producing some form of explanation, any explanation, for models that had previously offered none, and the field's early successes are appropriately measured against that comparatively modest bar. The field's current concerns, faithfulness validation, human evaluation, standardized benchmarking, all discussed in this chapter, reflect a maturing field that has moved past the question of whether explanation is possible at all and toward the harder, more consequential question of whether a given explanation can be trusted and acted on.

The framework presented in this book is positioned at this more mature stage of the field's development, building on the foundational gradient and concept-based techniques established earlier in the field's history while contributing the unified, fidelity-validated, and operationally grounded treatment that this more mature stage of the field increasingly demands. Readers entering this field for the first time through this book should understand that they are joining a research and engineering discipline still actively defining its own standards of rigor, not one that has already settled into a fixed, finished methodology.

CHAPTER 14.

Conclusion: Toward Trustworthy Image Intelligence

Introduction

This book opened with a simple observation: convolutional and generative adversarial networks have become extraordinarily capable at the tasks they were designed for, image classification and detection on one hand, realistic image synthesis on the other, while remaining largely opaque about how they arrive at any individual result. This concluding chapter draws together the threads developed across the preceding thirteen chapters and reflects on what the explainable CNN-GAN framework ultimately offers, and what its adoption requires of the organizations and practitioners who build on it.

Rather than introducing new technical material, this chapter revisits the framework's central claims, summarizes the evidence presented in support of them, and closes with a direct statement of what the authors believe a reader should take away from the book as a whole.

Structure

- Revisiting the Central Claims
- What the Evidence Supports
- What Adoption Requires
- Closing Reflection

Revisiting the Central Claims

The framework presented in this book rests on three claims, each developed at length in earlier chapters. First, that the explainability problem in discriminative image analytics, addressed by the explainable CNN module described in Chapter 5, and the explainability problem in generative image synthesis, addressed by the explainable GAN module described in Chapter 6, while differing substantially in their technical mechanics, share enough structural similarity that a unified explanation layer, described in Chapter 7, can meaningfully aggregate and present both within a single coherent view.

Second, that explainability need not come at the cost of predictive accuracy or generative quality severe enough to make the trade-off impractical for production use;

the experimental results presented in Chapter 9, in which the proposed framework's accuracy and FID scores remained close to those of the unexplained baseline models while its explainability score rose substantially, support this claim within the scope of the experimental setup described in that chapter, though the discussion in Section 9.4 was careful to note the conditions under which the trade-off could shift unfavorably.

Third, that explainability, properly instrumented, is not merely a compliance checkbox but an operationally useful signal, one that supports debugging, as discussed throughout Chapter 5, supports governance and regulatory readiness, as discussed in Chapter 12, and supports the kind of domain-expert trust that determines whether a technically sound system is actually adopted in practice, as the case studies in Chapter 11 illustrated across three different industry contexts.

What the Evidence Supports

The experimental evidence presented in Chapter 9, drawn from the methodology described in Chapter 8, supports the framework's core viability: a measurable, substantial gain in explainability score, from the low-to-mid sixties for an unexplained discriminative baseline and the mid-fifties for an unexplained generative baseline, to a unified score in the high seventies for the integrated framework, achieved with only a marginal reduction in classification accuracy and an essentially unchanged generative quality score as measured by FID.

The qualitative evidence presented in Section 9.3 and revisited in the case studies of Chapter 11 supports a complementary and arguably more important claim: that the quantitative explainability gain translates into explanations that domain experts in medical imaging, industrial inspection, and security and surveillance contexts found usable and informative, not merely numerically favorable on an abstract metric divorced from practical decision-making.

Together, this evidence supports treating the framework as a credible foundation for organizations seeking to deploy explainable image analytics and synthetic image generation in production, while the limitations and open research gaps discussed candidly throughout the book, particularly in Chapter 13, support treating the framework as a foundation to build on and extend rather than a finished, permanent solution to the explainability problem.

What Adoption Requires

Organizations considering adoption of the framework described in this book should expect the technical integration described in Chapter 10 to be the more tractable part of the undertaking. The explainable CNN and GAN modules, the unified explainability layer, and the supporting metrics described in Chapter 8 are designed to integrate into an existing MLOps pipeline with bounded, well-understood engineering effort.

The organizational and procedural commitments described in Chapter 12, establishing a governance process with real enforcement authority, building documentation discipline into the standard model lifecycle, and engaging domain experts in the concept curation work discussed in Chapter 13, generally represent the larger and more sustained undertaking, and are, in the authors' experience reflected throughout the case studies in Chapter 11, the difference between organizations that realize the framework's full operational value and those that adopt its technical components but treat explainability as a one-time audit exercise rather than a continuing operational discipline.

Practitioners approaching this material for the first time should treat Chapters 4 through 8 as the technical core to master, Chapters 9 through 12 as the evidentiary and operational grounding that justifies and guides real deployment, and Chapter 13 as a candid map of where the framework's current technical boundaries lie and where future extension is most likely to be needed.

Closing Reflection

The broader trajectory of image-based machine learning over the past decade has been one of steadily increasing capability, models that classify more accurately, generate more convincingly, and operate at greater scale with each successive generation. That trajectory has not been matched by an equally steady increase in the field's ability to explain what these increasingly capable systems are actually doing, and the gap between capability and explainability has, if anything, widened as architectures have grown more complex and generative models in particular have become more difficult to interpret through any single, simple lens.

The framework presented in this book is offered as one concrete, evidence-supported step toward closing that gap, not as a final word on the subject. The authors' hope, consistent with the philosophy carried forward from the discussion of observability and trust as first-class engineering concerns in the authors' earlier work on software delivery practices, is that readers will treat explainability not as an afterthought bolted onto a finished system, but as a design requirement considered from the earliest stages of building any system that classifies images, generates them, or, as is increasingly common, does both at once.

Image intelligence that cannot account for itself is, ultimately, intelligence that organizations, regulators, and the people affected by its decisions are right to view with caution. The work described across the preceding fourteen chapters is an argument, grounded in mathematics, experimental evidence, and field experience, that this caution need not be the final word, and that explainable, trustworthy image intelligence is an achievable engineering standard rather than an aspirational ideal.

What Success Would Look Like Five Years From Now

It is appropriate to close this book by offering a concrete picture of what success would look like if the framework and the broader research direction it represents continue to mature over the coming years. Success, in this book's view, would not necessarily mean universal adoption of this specific framework's particular technical choices; reconciliation algorithms, concept vocabularies, and fidelity metrics will all reasonably continue to evolve, and a framework frozen exactly as presented in this book's chapters would likely be superseded within a small number of years by improved successors, much as this book's own literature survey in Chapter 2 traced a comparable pattern of rapid supersession in the field's earlier history.

What this book hopes will prove more durable than its specific technical choices is the underlying principle that discriminative and generative explainability deserve to be treated as a single unified concern rather than as separate research tracks pursued by largely non-overlapping communities, and that explanation fidelity deserves the same systematic testing discipline that the field has long applied to predictive accuracy and generative quality. If readers of this book carry forward primarily that principle, adapting it to architectures, modalities, and deployment contexts well beyond what this book's specific chapters anticipated, the book will have succeeded in its central purpose regardless of how its particular algorithms have aged.

On the Relationship Between This Book and the Authors' Prior Work

Readers familiar with the authors' earlier published work on continuous integration and continuous delivery practices in modern software engineering will recognize a recurring theme connecting that earlier work to this book: a conviction that systems capable of autonomous, high-velocity action, whether a deployment pipeline pushing code to production multiple times a day or an image analytics framework classifying and generating images at scale, become more trustworthy, not less capable, when instrumented with the observability and explanatory infrastructure needed to account for their own behavior after the fact.

In the earlier work on delivery pipelines, that infrastructure took the form of build telemetry, deployment audit trails, and automated rollback criteria. In this book, it takes the form of attribution maps, concept activation scores, latent sensitivity profiles, and the unified explainability score formalized in Chapter 8. The specific technical vocabulary differs substantially between the two domains, but the underlying engineering philosophy, that velocity and accountability are complementary rather than competing system properties when the right instrumentation is built in from the start, is the same philosophy this book has applied throughout to the specific and increasingly consequential domain of explainable image intelligence.

A Final Word to Practitioners

For the practitioner who has worked through the preceding thirteen chapters with an eye toward an actual production deployment rather than purely theoretical interest, a few closing, practical reminders are worth restating outside the specific chapter context in which they first appeared. Begin with the explanation fidelity testing described in Section 8.5 before trusting any explanation method's output in a real deployment, regardless of how visually compelling that output appears on initial inspection. Engage domain experts in concept vocabulary curation, discussed in Chapter 5 and revisited in Chapter 13, from the earliest stages of a deployment rather than treating it as a refinement to be addressed after the technical pipeline is otherwise complete.

Build the governance and documentation discipline described in Chapter 12 into the standard model lifecycle from the first production deployment, rather than retrofitting it later once an audit or incident makes its absence painfully apparent, and revisit that governance process periodically through the kind of self-audit discussed in that chapter, rather than assuming that a process correct at the time it was established will remain correct indefinitely as the surrounding system and organization evolve.

Acknowledging the Limits of This Book

No single book can offer a complete, permanently current treatment of a research area as actively evolving as explainable artificial intelligence for image analytics and synthetic image generation, and this book does not claim to. The mathematical foundations presented in Chapter 8 and the framework architecture presented in Chapters 4 through 7 are intended to remain useful well beyond any single generation of underlying model architectures, since they are formulated at a level of abstraction that does not depend on the specific CNN backbone or GAN variant in use at the time of writing.

The specific experimental results presented in Chapter 9, the specific regulatory landscape discussed in Chapter 12, and the specific research frontier surveyed in Chapter 13, by contrast, are necessarily snapshots of a particular moment, and readers returning to this book at a substantially later date should treat those specific chapters as historically informative rather than as a current statement of best practice, while treating the framework's underlying architecture and mathematical foundations as the durable contribution this book is intended to offer.

About the Author

Dr. Gaurav Shekhar is Senior Leader, Enterprise AI Architect and Principal Technical Consultant at leading US Financial Services Organization, with over twenty years of experience across financial services technology, spanning AI and machine learning platforms, platform engineering, cloud transformation, and enterprise architecture. His engineering leadership has included large-scale fraud detection and observability platforms, on-premises to cloud migration programs, and the architecture of resilient, high-throughput payments systems during a prior senior payments architecture role at Discover Payments.

He is an IEEE Senior Member who actively organizes and participates in professional community events connecting practitioners across financial services, cloud infrastructure, and applied AI. He is the published author of two books on Cilium-eBPF and CICD for Platform Engineering, an active technical blogger on DZone and Medium, and a frequent conference speaker, including a recent session at Open Source North on eBPF and cloud-native security.

Dr Gaurav Shekhar earned his Honorary Doctorate from Kennedy University of Florida, USA due to his extraordinary contributions to Software Engineering and Cybersecurity Space.

He holds a patent pending in heterogeneous data source integration and analysis, and has published peer-reviewed research on explainable artificial intelligence for image analytics, the subject of this book. His work consistently returns to a single theme: that systems capable of acting autonomously at scale must also be capable of accounting for their own behavior, whether the system in question is a continuous delivery pipeline, a fraud detection platform, or, as in this book, a hybrid CNN-GAN image intelligence framework.

Readers can find his published research, technical writing, and professional profile through Google Scholar, DZone, and GitHub.

Glossary

The following terms recur throughout this book and are collected here for convenient reference, each with a pointer to the chapter in which it receives full treatment.

Attribution Map

A spatial visualization, typically overlaid on the original input image, indicating which regions of that image most strongly influenced a model's prediction, computed using gradient-based or perturbation-based techniques as described in Chapter 5.

Black-Box Problem

The general difficulty of understanding why a complex model, such as a deep CNN or GAN, produced a specific output, arising from the model's high dimensionality, nonlinearity, and depth, as introduced in Chapter 1.

Concept Activation Vector (CAV)

A direction in a CNN's internal activation space, computed using example images representing a human-interpretable concept, used to measure how strongly that concept influences a given prediction, as described in Chapter 5.

Disentanglement

The degree to which individual dimensions of a generative model's latent space each correspond to a single, independent, human-interpretable semantic attribute, discussed in Chapter 6.

Discriminator

The component of a generative adversarial network trained to distinguish real training images from synthetic images produced by the generator, as introduced in Chapter 1.

Explanation Fidelity

A measure of how faithfully an explanation reflects the actual internal computation of the model it explains, typically validated through stability testing under input or weight perturbation, formalized in Section 8.5.

Fréchet Inception Distance (FID)

A widely used quantitative metric for assessing the quality and diversity of images produced by a generative model, by comparing the statistical distribution of generated images to that of real images, referenced throughout Chapters 4 and 9.

Generative Adversarial Network (GAN)

A generative modeling architecture consisting of a generator and a discriminator trained in opposition to one another, introduced in Chapter 1 and treated in depth in Chapter 6.

Gradient-Based Attribution

A family of explainability techniques that compute an attribution map using the gradient of a model's output with respect to its input or intermediate activations, described in Chapter 5.

Latent Space

The compressed, lower-dimensional vector space from which a generative model, such as a GAN, produces output images, typically explored through sampling or interpolation, discussed in Chapter 6.

Latent Sensitivity Analysis

A technique for explaining a GAN's output by systematically perturbing individual dimensions of its latent input and observing the resulting change in the generated image, described in Chapter 6.

Mode Collapse

A GAN training failure in which the generator produces a narrow range of outputs rather than capturing the full diversity of the training data distribution, referenced in Chapter 1.

Post-Hoc Explanation

An explanation method applied to a model after it has already been trained, without requiring modification to the model's architecture or training procedure, contrasted with intrinsic explainability in Chapter 2.

Saliency Map

An early and foundational form of gradient-based attribution map, highlighting input pixels that most strongly influence a model's output, referenced in Chapters 2 and 5.

TCAV (Testing with Concept Activation Vectors)

A specific methodology for quantifying how much a given human-interpretable concept influences a model's predictions across a class, using concept activation vectors, described in Chapter 5.

Unified Explainability Layer

The component of the framework presented in this book responsible for normalizing, aggregating, and presenting explanation signals from both the CNN and GAN modules within a single coherent view, described in Chapter 7.

Unified Explainability Score

A formal, composite metric introduced in this book for measuring the overall explainability of a hybrid CNN-GAN system, combining attribution fidelity, concept interpretability, and latent interpretability signals, formalized in Section 8.6.

Appendix A: Reference Summary

This appendix consolidates reference material referenced throughout the preceding chapters: a complete list of the source research this book builds on, and a summary table of the experimental results presented in Chapter 9, reproduced here for convenient reference without the surrounding discussion.

A.1 Performance Comparison Summary (Chapter 9)

Table A.1: Summary of the experimental comparison presented in full in Chapter 9.

Model	Accuracy (%)	FID	Explainability Score
CNN (Baseline)	92.4	—	61
GAN (Baseline)	—	28.7	54
Proposed XAI Framework	91.8	29.3	79

A.2 Source Research and Further Reading

Appendix B: Plain-Language Notation Reference

This second appendix collects plain-language translations of the principal formal definitions introduced in Chapter 8, intended as a ready reference for practitioners preparing stakeholder-facing materials for audiences who do not require, or do not wish to work through, the full mathematical notation. Each entry pairs the formal concept with a short, non-technical restatement suitable for inclusion in an executive summary, a compliance memo, or a model documentation card.

Attribution Fidelity Bound

A guarantee about how closely an explanation's claimed important regions match the regions the model actually relied on, expressed as a worst-case bound rather than an average-case tendency.

Concept Interpretability Score

A measure of how cleanly the model's internal reasoning maps onto human-understandable concepts, such as named visual features a domain expert would recognize, rather than uninterpretable internal statistics.

Latent Interpretability Score

A measure of how many of a generative model's internal control dimensions correspond to a single recognizable visual change, as opposed to dimensions that change multiple visual properties simultaneously in a way no human would describe with one word.

Unified Explainability Score

A single combined number intended to summarize, at a glance, how explainable a hybrid CNN-GAN system is overall, built by combining the three preceding scores under the weighting scheme described in Chapter 8.

Deletion-Based Faithfulness Metric

A test that progressively hides the pixels an explanation claims are most important and checks whether the model's confidence drops accordingly; a faithful explanation should cause a large, early confidence drop.

Insertion-Based Faithfulness Metric

The mirror image of the deletion-based test: pixels claimed most important are progressively revealed, and a faithful explanation should cause confidence to rise quickly.

Explanation Fidelity Testing Protocol

The combined automated-and-human review process this book recommends running before trusting any explanation method in a production deployment, rather than trusting a method simply because it is popular or intuitive.

Appendix C: Expanded Implementation Checklist

This appendix provides an expanded implementation checklist intended for engineering teams beginning a production rollout of the framework described in this book, organized by project phase rather than by book chapter, to mirror how most teams actually plan deployment work.

Phase 1: Foundation

Confirm the underlying CNN and GAN models meet the baseline performance thresholds discussed in Chapter 9 before investing in explainability tooling; freeze the explanation output schema described in Chapter 7 as an early cross-team contract; identify which of the case study patterns in Chapter 10 most closely matches your deployment domain.

Phase 2: Instrumentation

Implement gradient-based attribution and concept activation vector extraction for the CNN module per Chapter 5; implement latent sensitivity analysis for the GAN module per Chapter 6; verify both modules' raw outputs independently before attempting reconciliation.

Phase 3: Reconciliation

Implement the unified explanation layer's normalization and aggregation logic per Chapter 7; run the explanation fidelity testing protocol from Chapter 8 on a representative validation sample; calibrate the human-review sampling rate to your deployment's stakes level.

Phase 4: Rollout

Sequence team-by-team adoption per the staged approach in Chapter 11; establish the leading indicators for explainability value discussed in Chapter 10 before, not after, full production launch; schedule a post-launch retrospective at a fixed interval rather than leaving it open-ended.

www.ingramcontent.com/pod-product-compliance
Lightning Source LLC
LaVergne TN
LVHW021746071126
851857LV00039B/942
* 9 7 9 8 8 9 9 6 6 6 6 9 8 *